Cambridge Elements ≡

Elements in the Philosophy of Biology
edited by
Grant Ramsey
KU Leuven
Michael Ruse
Florida State University

BIOLOGICAL ORGANIZATION

Leonardo Bich
University of the Basque Country (UPV/EHU)

CAMBRIDGE
UNIVERSITY PRESS

Shaftesbury Road, Cambridge CB2 8EA, United Kingdom

One Liberty Plaza, 20th Floor, New York, NY 10006, USA

477 Williamstown Road, Port Melbourne, VIC 3207, Australia

314–321, 3rd Floor, Plot 3, Splendor Forum, Jasola District Centre,
New Delhi – 110025, India

103 Penang Road, #05–06/07, Visioncrest Commercial, Singapore 238467

Cambridge University Press is part of Cambridge University Press & Assessment,
a department of the University of Cambridge.

We share the University's mission to contribute to society through the pursuit of
education, learning and research at the highest international levels of excellence.

www.cambridge.org
Information on this title: www.cambridge.org/9781009539401

DOI: 10.1017/9781009393959

First published 2024

A catalogue record for this publication is available from the British Library

ISBN 978-1-009-53940-1 Hardback
ISBN 978-1-009-39396-6 Paperback
ISSN 2515-1126 (online)
ISSN 2515-1118 (print)

Cambridge University Press & Assessment has no responsibility for the persistence
or accuracy of URLs for external or third-party internet websites referred to in this
publication and does not guarantee that any content on such websites is, or will
remain, accurate or appropriate.

Biological Organization

Elements in the Philosophy of Biology

DOI: 10.1017/9781009393959
First published online: December 2024

Leonardo Bich
University of the Basque Country (UPV/EHU)
Author for correspondence: Leonardo Bich, leonardo.bich@ehu.eus

Abstract: Living systems are complex systems made of components that tend to degrade, but nonetheless they maintain themselves far from equilibrium. This requires living systems to extract energy and materials from the environment and use them to build and repair their parts by regulating their activities based on their internal and external conditions in ways that allow them to keep living. The philosophical and theoretical approach discussed in this Element aims to explain these features of biological systems by appealing to their organization. It addresses classical and more recent issues in philosophy of biology, from origins and definitions of life to biological teleology and functions, from an original perspective mainly focused on the living system, its physiology and behavior, rather than evolution. It discusses and revises the conceptual foundations of this approach and presents an updated version of it. This title is also available as Open Access on Cambridge Core.

Keywords: organization, autonomy, control, mechanism, organisms

ISBNs: 9781009539401 (HB), 9781009393966 (PB), 9781009393959 (OC)
ISSNs: 2515-1126 (online), 2515-1118 (print)

Contents

1 Introduction: Understanding What Makes a System Living

Organisms are complex systems made of soft materials that tend to degrade, but they maintain themselves through the constant turnover of their components. At first glance, they might seem very fragile compared to other natural systems or to human-made artifacts. Artifacts, for example, can have very resistant parts, which can remain unchanged for a long time. Organisms, instead, are subject to the constant degradation and transformation of their components, which need to be continuously replaced or repaired. They are made of components, such as proteins, which are highly dynamic, have a short lifespan and are constantly transformed. Proteins spontaneously degrade, or they can lose their functional shape (denaturation) due to changes in the properties of their surroundings such as temperature, pH, and interactions with other molecules. Moreover, they can be degraded by the organisms when they cannot perform their activity anymore or such activity is not needed, and their parts can be recycled to build new proteins. Another important difference is that while entities like rocks or even most artifacts can just persist for a very long time without performing any activity, living organisms cannot shut down their own processes – apart from extreme cases such as bacterial spores, and even in those case only partially – but on the contrary, they need to procure nutrients from which to extract the energy and matter necessary to run their metabolism, to ensure the turnover of their parts, or to move in and interact with their environment.

Despite the fragility of their components and the need to continuously act (or, better, by virtue of these properties), individual organisms and life on Earth more generally, exhibit remarkable resilience. While artifacts, once damaged, stay so and cannot function, living organisms, instead, can repair or replace their parts. They can shut down some of their more demanding activities and mobilize their resources to respond to stress, and they can recover from severe damages. Importantly, while artifacts are made to work under a fixed set of conditions – although in recent trends the aim is to design more flexible artifacts – organisms can function in different ways under different conditions. It is thanks to these capabilities that plants can survive herbicides and can grow in areas contaminated by toxic waste, or that bacteria can resist antibiotics and can live in almost all environments from the stratosphere to the depths of the Earth crust, under a variety of conditions that include extreme temperatures, pH, pressure, and so on. Together with plants, fungi, and unicellular organisms, animal life was even able to survive the consequences of the impacts of asteroids.

Organisms, taken individually or in groups, exhibit a great flexibility that allows them to cope with continuously changing conditions in their environment but also within themselves. For example, they can modify their internal physiology or their behavior depending on changes in the environmental temperature (Hagen, 2021) or in the type and amounts of food available (e.g. synthesizing different enzymes to digest different sources of nutrients), on the specific phase of their life cycle (e.g. growth, migration, reproduction, etc.), on the presence of prey or predators, on the state of other organisms, and on the presence of light or darkness.

Let us illustrate this by briefly mentioning three examples of radical changes adopted by relatively simple organisms. The first is the case of Choanoflagellates of the species *Salpingoeca rosetta*: eukaryotic organisms that can live as free unicellular systems. In response to diverse environmental cues, they can change their way of living, and adopt multicellular modes of association by forming simple chains or spherical colonies kept together by cytoplasmatic bridges and extracellular matrix (Larson et al., 2020). The second example is related to the presence or absence of light. The cycle of light and darkness can determine when to look for prey or whether it is safe to move about in the environment. It can also influence metabolic activities. An interesting case of the capability of adapting to the presence and absence of light is circadian rhythms, which can be identified in many living organisms, from bacteria to plants and animals. Let us focus on bacteria. They are very small organisms. The internal space and the energy available to them are very limited. In photosynthetic bacteria such as cyanobacteria, keeping photosynthesis mechanisms at work during the day is an important source of energy, but during darkness is a waste of resources. Moreover, the oxygen produced by photosynthesis is toxic to the enzyme nitrogenase, involved in nitrogen fixation, another important activity necessary for their maintenance. Therefore, these two different processes, photosynthesis and nitrogen fixation, need to be kept separate. These two activities are usually performed by different organisms. However, the cyanobacterium *Synechococcus* can do both activities by segregating photosynthesis and nitrogen fixation in time: day and night, respectively. Its circadian clock can keep track of light–dark cycles in its environment and activate the expression of different genes accordingly, thus modulating its physiological activities (Cohen & Golden, 2015; Bechtel & Bich, 2021). The third example concerns changes on the basis of the state of other organisms. From bacteria to fungi, plants, and animals, living systems employ a variety of strategies and mechanisms that allow them to communicate with one another and coordinate their activities, including metabolism, foraging, and reproductive behavior. A basic case is *quorum sensing* in bacteria. It involves individual bacteria synthesizing and releasing into the environment a molecule, an autoinducer, while sensing and responding to the concentration of that same molecule in their surroundings. The bond between these signaling molecules and their bacterial receptors activates the expression of several genes, including those involved in the synthesis of these same signal molecules. In this way, when more bacteria respond to the concentration registered by their own receptors by producing more autoinducers, the signal is amplified. *Quorum sensing* provides a way for individual bacteria to regulate their activities depending on the number and state of other bacteria available nearby, whether of the same species or of other species, thus allowing them to coordinate activities such as aggregation, the formation, growth and disassembly of biofilms, and collective movement.

These are just a few examples of the fact that, even in their most basic forms, living organisms, despite their apparent fragility (and the fragility of their parts), can exhibit remarkable resilience and versatility. One of the reasons is that – unlike human artifacts, which are produced from without – living systems have the capability to produce, repair, transform, and replace their parts. The other reason is that organisms do not just replace and repair their parts. They also modify themselves and what they do on the basis of their internal physiological state and environmental conditions. They are not just alive but employ a variety of activities that allow them to keep living. These two properties, self-production and self-regulation, go hand in hand: Organisms maintain themselves alive and they can do so because they are constantly changing.

These capabilities, as we observe them now, can be understood as the result of a long history of evolution by natural selection, which took place over a span of more than three billion years since the origin of life – not including prebiotic evolution, where the main features that characterize unicellular organisms have been established – and produced continuous lineages of organisms. However, it is important to consider that, in turn, it is the very ability of each given organism to maintain itself and keep living under different and often threatening conditions that has allowed its survival and reproduction in its environment, and therefore made evolution possible. While not denying the importance and role of evolutionary considerations, a possible research avenue to understand these distinctive features of living organisms is to investigate how organisms, rather than their lineages, are maintained, by focusing on their physiologies and behaviors.

The philosophical and theoretical framework discussed in this Element aims to do so by explaining these features of biological systems in terms of their organization. This framework characterizes a biological organism as a system capable of producing its own components, regulating its activities, and maintaining itself while interacting with its environment. To explain this capacity, this tradition appeals to the internal organization of the organism, which is maintained despite the continuous transformations that the organism undergoes at the level of its components. According to the advocates of this approach, it is the organization of a system – that is, the set of relations between its components, rather than the properties of specific components – that defines it as a system of a particular class and that needs to be maintained for the system to keep its identity as a member of that class (Maturana & Varela, 1980: xx). In the case of living systems, the organization to be maintained is the one connecting production and transformation processes, and the activities of the components of a living system. This specific organization makes the system able to synthesize the very components that make it up, and run its internal processes, by using energy and matter from the environment. This organization is often called "autonomous" (Varela, 1979; Moreno & Mossio, 2015), because by realizing it living systems are considered as the source of their own activities and through such activities they contribute, at least in part, to their own existence (see Sections 3–5).

Inspired by the work of Claude Bernard, and by Cybernetics, Systems Theory, and Theoretical Biology, the organizational framework was built upon pioneering work on biological organization (also known under the label of "biological autonomy tradition") carried out by Jean Piaget (1967), Robert Rosen (1972), Humberto Maturana and Francisco Varela (Varela et al., 1974), and Howard Pattee (1972). More recently it has been further developed, among others, by Stuart Kauffman (2000) and by Alvaro Moreno and collaborators (e.g. Moreno & Mossio, 2015). Work based on the organizational perspective is gaining traction and has been raising increased interest in the past few years. This framework is being applied in the philosophy of biology to a wide range of topics, spanning from origins and definitions of life to biological teleology and functions, and to biological explanations. One of its distinctive features is that it addresses classical and more recent issues in the philosophy of biology from an original perspective mainly focused on the organism, its physiology and behavior, rather than evolution.

The Element presents and discusses the core ideas of this framework and how they originated. It revises its conceptual foundations and provides an updated view that analyzes in detail how these ideas are being developed by recent and current research – from the introduction of the notion of closure of constraint to that of regulatory control – and are being applied in the philosophy of biology. Section 2 clarifies the differences between this and other uses of the notion of organization in the philosophy of biology, such as network motifs and organizing or design principles. Section 3 analyzes the main attempts to develop a framework able to capture the distinctive features of biological organization, from the notion of autopoiesis to that of closure of constraints. Section 4 discusses recent work focused on regulatory control aimed at revising the conceptual core of the framework and overcoming some of the simplifications or limitations of previous accounts. It further develops this framework from an idea of organization based on the production, repair, and replacement of the parts, to one that includes the integration and modulation of their activities and explains the versatility of living organisms. Section 5 discusses applications of the organizational framework to philosophical issues such as biological teleology and functions. Section 6 addresses applications of this framework to specific biological phenomena such as origins of life and biological communication, which exemplify some of the core operational and explanatory features of this framework. Section 7 puts this framework into a wider context by discussing the relationships between this research tradition and new mechanism in producing biological explanations. Section 8 introduces the reader to some open challenges to this approach, coming from the debates on biological individuality and symbiosis and on the role of the environment, and sketches possible ways to address them.

2 Different Uses of Organization: Organizational Motifs, Organizing Principles, and the Organizational Framework

This section distinguishes between different, yet closely related, ways of talking about biological organization. It addresses three examples: organizational motifs, organizing or design principles, and the organizational framework. Before discussing their features and differences, let us focus first on what they have in common: a general idea of organization, common origins, and some common epistemic roles.

The term "organization" generally refers to the structure of relations between the parts of a given system or of a subsystem of a larger system, be they components, their activities, or processes. Together with reference to the types of components, organization is often used to characterize a system as an entity of a given class: For example, depending on how they are spatially organized, wooden parts can constitute a chair or a table, and mechanical parts a motorcycle or a car. Organization can mean different things in different contexts (physical, chemical, biological, in artifacts, etc.) and it can refer to different types of relations: for example, spatial ones, like in the map of a subway system, or temporal, such as in a succession of events. Each domain of investigation makes different distinctions when identifying a system: Different kinds of relations are considered as pertinent in order to describe the phenomena object of study, and different operations of partition are performed in order to extract the relevant components. Let us think, for example, of how many system domains can be found in a human body: from molecular and cellular ones to complexes of organs (e.g. the digestive or the vascular system), up to ecosystems such as the gut, populated by our bacterial symbionts. As a consequence, the same material entity can in principle be described in terms of different kinds of systems, each with specific components and organization.

The way organization has been addressed in biology by the theoretical tradition discussed in this Element is in causal terms: as a pattern of causal connectivity. A causal account of organization, as discussed by Levy and Bechtel (2013: 243), "involves an internal division of labor whereby different components perform different causal roles." Systems that do not involve differential causal roles for their components are not organized. Causal connectivity can be characterized in different ways: for example, in terms of how parts and processes produce a particular output of a system, in terms of the degree of connectivity between the parts of a system, and so on.

Current uses of the notion of organization in biology are mainly grounded in two closely interconnected research traditions of the twentieth century: Cybernetics and System Theory. Both traditions can be characterized as attempts to cut across disciplinary fields to take inspirations from different phenomena and favor the exchange of concepts and models. These traditions, often overlapping, have the ultimate goal of studying concepts and building research tools that can be fruitfully applied to study and intervene in a wide range of phenomena from heterogeneous fields, but that exhibit some common abstract features. For these reasons, Cybernetics and Systems Theory have been characterized by the participation of researchers from a wide range of disciplines.

The term "cybernetics" was coined in the late forties of the twentieth century (Wiener, 1948), as the science of "steersmanship" or control (from the ancient Greek word "kybernetes," which means steersman). It was established as a research tradition in the context of the Macy Conferences, a series of interdisciplinary conferences that were held at the Josiah Macy Jr. Foundation in New York from 1946 to 1953 (McCulloch, 1974; Pias, 2016). Since then, it has been focused on two main activities: (1) the study of patterns of organization common to different phenomena, usually subsystems of a larger system; (2) the development of formal descriptions of these patterns of connectivity that could be applied in different disciplines, from engineering to biology, psychology, neurophysiology, and social sciences (Wiener, 1948; Ashby, 1956; Pickering, 2010).

This approach has been employed in different directions, such as for example the application of mathematical logic to study the functioning of the nervous system and to show how the nervous system could implement formal logic, and the development of information theory and computing machines. One of the main foci has been on the study and formalization of feedback mechanisms to understand control and stabilization in biological systems and human-made machines. Negative feedback describes phenomena in which the value of the output of a system is used to modify the activity of the system (the output "feeds back") in such a way as to create a loop that reduces fluctuations in the output itself, and to maintain its value stable within a specific range.[1] Feedback mechanisms are characterized by a distinctive pattern of connections: a circular causal relation between a controller and a controlled subsystem. The controller is a sensory-effector subsystem that senses both the external inputs to the system and the outputs of the controlled subsystem, and acts as an effector on the controlled subsystem by modifying its activity. The loop is established because the outputs of the controller are the inputs of the controlled subsystem, and in turn, the outputs of the controlled subsystem are part of the inputs of the controller. Feedback mechanisms are control devices that, although not specific to biology, have become since the thirties an important tool in different areas of biology (e.g. neurophysiology, see for instance McCulloch, 1974), often in association with the idea of homeostasis (Cannon, 1929). Since then, they have been used to model and understand dynamically stable situations in which the value of a variable appears to be actively maintained within a given range. The main strategy employed to study them has been to analyze the technological mechanisms of stabilization in artifacts to advance hypotheses on the functioning of biological ones and vice versa to exploit the knowledge of the latter for the implementation of the former.

Although they share the core idea, different models vary in terms of the number and kind of elements constituting negative feedback mechanisms. One may be familiar with a thermostat, a device that measures the temperature of a space such as a room and, depending on the deviation of the measured temperature from a value set by the user, it activates or deactivates an effector device, such as a heater, so as to keep the room temperature stable. Let us consider a basic but illustrative example of biological negative feedback, the case of allosteric feedback inhibition (Figure 1), discovered and conceptualized by Monod et al. (1963) in molecular biology. Allosteric control is the change in the shape and functioning of a protein (inhibition or activation) due to the interaction with an effector molecule in a site different from the active one where catalysis takes place. Given a metabolic pathway with supply of reactants from the outside (the input) in which reactions at each step ($A{\to}B$, $B{\to}C$, ... $\to N$) are catalyzed by a different type of enzymes (E, E', E" ... En), a feedback loop of allosteric inhibition is realized when the enzymes E, which for example catalyze the reaction $A{\to}B$, are allosterically inhibited by one of the products of this pathway: a metabolite N. As a result, when the concentration of N is above a given threshold, the activities of Es are inhibited and so is the pathway responsible for the production of N, thus avoiding the accumulation of this metabolite in the

---

[1] Under specific conditions, feedback loops can themselves create fluctuations or oscillations: a capacity often employed to create and sustain rhythmic phenomena.

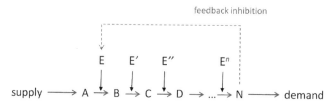

Figure 1 A basic example of negative feedback loop from molecular biology: allosteric feedback inhibition in a metabolic pathway. The catalytic activity of an enzyme E in the pathway is inhibited by the interaction with a metabolite N, which is produced in the pathway (from Bich et al., 2016, reproduced with permission from Springer Nature).

system. A pathway so organized with a negative feedback mechanism realizes a loop where the components E, the controllers, can change their conformation and exhibit at least two possible states, active or inhibited, when free or bound to N respectively. The components E act as both sensors of the value of the controlled variable N (at the allosteric site) and effectors (at the catalytic site) acting on the process of production of N.

The core approach of Cybernetics is to establish isomorphisms between patterns of connectivity, such as feedback loops, common to different systems, and to develop general abstract tools to study, model, or design them. The main idea underlying the cybernetic tradition is that what is responsible for a given behavior or phenomenon is the way of connecting components, and this can be shared by different types of systems regardless of their material realization. It is such an organization, more than the underlying physical structure, which would provide the means to understand, model, and design a phenomenon. This is exactly what allows cyberneticians to transfer models from one domain to another: abstracting from the intrinsic properties of the material components of a specific physical instantiation of a mechanism such as a feedback loop (from a thermostat to allosteric inhibition, to physiological phenomena such as the regulation of glycemia or the control of body temperature, of blood oxygen, etc.) to focus on the modes of causal connections between the parts.

General Systems Theory refers, broadly speaking, to a more general framework mainly aiming at the development of an integrated, unified science of wholeness and organization, into which cybernetics can also be integrated (see also Pouvreau & Drack, 2007). Its roots can be traced back to the thirties of the twentieth century with the studies conducted by Ludwig von Bertalanffy on developmental processes and on living organisms as thermodynamically open systems, which ascribe an important role to organization and more precisely to the nonlinear interactions between components. Developed in close parallel with Cybernetics, its theoretical foundations were laid in the late sixties (von Bertalanffy, 1968; Klir, 1991).

One of the central tenets of General System Theory is that in order to understand a system one has to consider it in its totality, rather than as a sum of preexisting components. According to von Bertalanffy, the reason for this is that the relations between the components modify their behaviors, giving rise to global emergent properties and phenomena that cannot be found by studying the individual components. The main research lines in this tradition include: the search for "laws of organization" governing emergent phenomena in which the behavior of parts depends on the whole; the study of general properties of systems; discussion of the differences between organisms and machines;[2] and the study of the dynamic nature of organisms as essentially active systems, which respond to external stimuli through structural changes. The goal is to find homologies between different types of phenomena that share, like to those studied by cybernetics, some common abstract features independent of the specific properties of the material parts, and to develop a common perspective for different sciences.

General System Theory pursues the unification of sciences by developing general approaches that do not imply reduction to a more fundamental science. Its approach consists instead of developing a common perspective, with a shared vocabulary and invariant concepts, tools, and laws applicable across different fields that favor exchanges of ideas, questions, and solutions between disciplines. Examples of these special systems laws, which in principle depend on organization, include the exponential law for growth,[3] Shannon theorem about the maximum amount of information that can be transmitted through a channel, or Ashby's principle of requisite variety for control systems, according to which in order to block all possible perturbations a controller needs to have at least as many possible states as the environment or the other subsystems with which it is going to interact.

In sum, Cybernetics is focused on pinpointing specific patterns of organization such as feedback loops, establishing isomorphisms between specific instances of them by means of abstract mathematical tools, and then applying them to specific cases by adding more details. General Systems Theory,

---

[2] This is an important difference with Cybernetics, which was focused instead on identifying and investigating similarities between organisms and machines with the aim to establish exchanges of concepts and models between these two different domains and develop new research lines and applications.

[3] An example is the growth of a population of bacteria in the presence of food. Bacteria reproduce by division and the number of bacteria doubles at each generation. The number of new bacteria is therefore proportional to the present population, and it increases at each new generation.

instead, aims to unify: to develop higher-order laws and general principles that can bring together descriptions and inform theoretical thinking (Green & Wolkenhauer, 2013).

The different uses of the notion of organization at work today in biology and philosophy of biology, such as organizational motifs, organizational or design principles, and the organizational framework, all share these common origins in Cybernetics and Systems Theory and the core idea of organization as a pattern of causal connections. However, each puts more emphasis on different aspects of this heritage. The distinction between them is not always clear-cut, as their uses often tend to overlap. Nonetheless they differ in scale, purpose, and epistemic role. Their discussion here is not exhaustive but aims to clarify their uses and put the organizational framework into perspective.

One way to talk of organization in biology is in terms of motifs of connectivity. This refers to the way processes and components are wired in small networks, such as different types of negative feedback loops. The aim is to understand the type of behavior a circuit thus obtained may exhibit. This approach closely follows the Cybernetic tradition and focuses on studying local patterns of connectivity, modeling them, and establishing isomorphisms between their instances in different systems. An example of this approach is Uri Alon's work on biological circuits in systems biology. This work is aimed at identifying and modeling mathematically local wiring patterns ("network motifs") in different biological phenomena (Alon, 2007). It is mainly focused on gene transcription networks, in which transcription factors encoded by a gene affect the transcription rate of another gene. Alon describes them in organizational terms as graphs in which nodes are the parts (the genes), and the edges are causal interactions (the modulation of transcription rates of other genes). Studying these transcription networks, Alon identifies what he calls "network motifs," that is, a small set of patterns that occur in actual networks significantly more often than in randomized networks. He then hypothesizes that the reason why these motifs are recurrent in a genome and are common to different organisms[4] is that they must enable the component elements to perform specific activities that are important for the system. Therefore, they need to be further studied and modeled.

These small circuits constitute the building blocks from which larger networks are built. Scientists can identify them based on their recurrence, and describe and compare their properties and function through mathematical modeling. Then they can see if the same motifs appear in other biological networks and apply the same

---

[4] They have been studied for example in model organisms such as the bacterium *Escherichia coli* or the eukaryotic yeast *Saccharomyces cerevisiae*.

modeling tools to understand their behaviors. Examples of this are protein modifications in signal transduction networks, or networks of synaptic connection in the worm *Caenorhabditis elegans* (Alon, 2007).

Organizing or design principles, as discussed by Green and Wolkenhauer (2013), instead refer to robust generalizations that aim to capture "dynamic and functional relations in a class of systems" without the details of a concrete mechanism in a specific context. They are wider and more general notions than motifs, and they usually refer to properties exhibited by larger organized systems rather than specific circuits. A paradigmatic example is Cannon's notion of *homeostasis*, that is, the capability of a physiological system to resist perturbations by maintaining some of its variables (e.g. pH, temperature, etc.) stable within a narrow range or, more generally, its internal conditions in a steady state.[5] Another principle is *optimality*, which is the capability of a biological system to maximize or minimize some function under given constraints. An example is the vascular system, considered as organized in each species in such a way as to maximize blood flow.

Organizing principles, in line with the tradition of General System Theory, provide explanations of how certain classes of organized systems work in principle and exhibit some general properties. However, they do not necessarily take the form of unifying general laws such as those pursued by General System Theory, but of pragmatic generalizations. They constitute sketches of explanations that abstract from details while focusing on some essential dynamics, used to build more detailed explanations in specific cases. Generalization across systems is then achieved by identifying what fundamental principles, such as optimality or homeostasis, some systems have in common, by investigating why they do so (e.g. whether they share some underlying mechanisms or a common dynamic behavior), and by developing modeling tools (Green & Jones, 2016).

Organizational motifs and organizing principles differ in the degree of generality and their focus on organizational building blocks and general properties, respectively. However, due to their shared focus on organization rather than material details, they exhibit common elements such as abstraction and decontextualization of certain mechanisms and properties. This allows scientists to develop epistemic tools for cross-disciplinary exchanges and applications and for the discovery of similar phenomena in other systems.

Lastly, let us look at a third use of the notion of organization in biology: the organizational framework. It differs from the other two approaches discussed in

---

[5] Organizing principles may include motifs, such as feedback, as special cases. Homeostasis, for example, can be realized through (multiple) negative feedback loops, but also by other means such as buffers, so that it does not coincide with one specific motif.

this section, in that the object of interest is not part of a network or a given property of a system, but the whole living organism. This approach brings together the quest for the generality of systems theory and the focus on patterns of connections of cybernetics under a different aim: to characterize the distinctive pattern of connectivity of a whole biological organization.[6] The primary focus here is on developing a theory that integrates into a coherent picture different principles, phenomena, mechanisms, and properties in the context of the organism. Abstraction is still very important but is pursued in a different sense, by identifying what is common to all living systems despite their material differences.

The origin of this attitude can be traced back, for example, to the theoretical work on Relational Biology carried out by Nicholas Rashevsky (1954) at the crossroads of Cybernetic and Systems Theory. His purpose was to develop a mathematical theory able to treat the integrated activity of the organism as a whole. According to Rashevsky, this can be achieved by looking for the minimal network of connections between biological properties that is common to all living organisms. Like cyberneticians, he is interested in establishing isomorphisms between different instances of a given type of organization. However, he does not look at local patterns such as feedback loops, but he focuses instead on finding isomorphisms between whole organisms, and identifying which basic relations are preserved. This approach is built on three assumptions: (1) the crucial importance of relations over material details, (2) the need to focus on the minimal set of relations between parts realized in all organisms, and (3) the possibility to study living systems starting from their common organization. He does not provide a hypothesis regarding the shape taken by this organization, but he suggests proceeding bottom-up by identifying sets of basic functions in different organisms and connecting them to describe how they are related. The common relations resulting from mapping one relational diagram to another would be the hypothetical relational structure of the minimal organization common to all living systems.

This is a distinctive way to think about biological organization. It aims to abstract from the multitude of structural components and processes to identify the minimal pattern of connectivity that makes a system a living organism, and it aims to use it to provide a theoretical understanding of biological systems. The next sections discuss how the organizational framework develops this approach in a distinctive way.

---

[6] As will be explained in detail in the next section, unlike cybernetics the organizational framework puts a special emphasis on the generative relations involved in the production of the system and its parts.

3 Biological Organization as a Self-Maintaining Causal Regime: From Autopoiesis to Closure of Constraints

The idea at the foundation of the organizational framework is that living systems are capable of constructing, repairing, transforming, and maintaining their parts, and consequently themselves, and they do so by using matter and energy extracted from their environment. The organizational framework was built upon the contributions of numerous theorists in the late sixties and early seventies including Jean Piaget (1967), Robert Rosen (1972), Humberto Maturana and Francisco Varela (Varela et al., 1974), and Tibor Ganti (1975), who have emphasized the importance of self-maintenance, characterized in terms of production and renovation of components.[7] To explain the capacity of biological systems to persist despite the turnover of very fragile and dynamic components such as proteins, this tradition appeals to the internal organization of the organism. This is what is maintained despite the continuous transformations that the organism undergoes at the level of its part. Due to the emphasis on the capacity of living systems to build and maintain themselves from within, this research line has also been known as the tradition of "biological autonomy" (Varela, 1979): to quote Kauffman (2000), in virtue of these properties living systems are autonomous because they are capable of "acting on their own behalf" without being completely driven by external factors.

These ideas were developed with the aim to build a new perspective in theoretical biology focused on providing an understanding of what living systems and their distinctive features are. One aim was to identify the differences between living systems and physico-chemical dynamical systems capable of persisting in time and of generating ordered structures, such as dissipative structures described in physics by Prigogine and collaborators (Glansdorff & Prigogine, 1971). The other aim was to provide an alternative approach to mainstream evolutionary and molecular biology, which were focused on two levels of description: the level of populations, lineages and species, and the molecular level. According to organizational theorists both these approaches were missing what they considered the fundamental biological level, that is, the one of living systems considered as the most basic biological units (Bich & Damiano, 2007). In this view, while theoretical work at the evolutionary level was presupposing systems capable of maintaining their viability in their environments and reproducing (Maturana & Varela, 1987), the work in molecular biology tended to identify properties and behaviors of biological systems with those of their molecular components, mainly the genome (Maturana, 1978: 30). Consistent with their roots in the traditions

---

[7] For historical analyses of this tradition, see Bich and Damiano (2008) and Letelier et al. (2011).

of cybernetics and systems theory, these theorists focused instead on what they considered the central biological level: the organization of living systems. These ideas were precursors of and in most cases have even directly inspired the renewed interest in systems and organisms that has characterized theoretical biology since the beginning of the twenty-first century (Gilbert & Sarkar, 2000; Woese, 2004; Cornish-Bowden, 2006; Etxeberria & Umerez, 2006; Bich & Damiano, 2008; Nicholson, 2014). However, as pointed out by Mossio, despite this new systemic trend, "organization still remains a blind spot of biological thinking" (Mossio, 2023: 1).

The main objective of the early contributors to the organizational framework was to develop concepts that identify and characterize aspects common to all actual and possible manifestations of life, thereby revealing the features of living systems that distinguish them from other classes of natural and artificial systems. According to this framework, these features cannot be found in the basic components of living systems (their material constitution or "structure") but in the ways these are related. The main reasons are two: (1) the same components can participate in other kinds of systems, and (2) biological systems are characterized by the fact that components are constantly produced, transformed, and degraded while the system as a whole persists. According to early organizational theorists, focusing on the properties of individual components risked leaving aside what makes the organism an integrated unity. This thesis was advanced in sharp opposition to mainstream molecular biology, represented by the theoretical and experimental work carried out by Francois Jacob and Jacques Monod (Jacob, 1970; Monod, 1970), who focused on the intrinsic properties of the material components of living systems: especially one component, the DNA, which was singled out as the main if not the only component responsible for the activity and reproduction of the organism.

The core feature of this approach is the focus on organization, that is, on the identification of the relations between the operations of components and between the processes of transformation carried out within a system. In this view, organization refers specifically to the way production and transformation processes are connected so that they are able to synthesize the very components that make them up. The fundamental feature of the organization of biological self-maintaining systems is its circular topology as a network of processes of production of components that in turn realize and maintain the network itself. This feature is captured by the term *autopoiesis*, from the Greek *"autos"* (self) and *"poiesis"* (production/creation): a regime of self-production or self-creation in which the output of the activity of the system is the system itself (Varela et al., 1974). As explained by Maturana (1980: 48): "The living organization is a circular organization which secures the production and maintenance of the components that specify it in such a manner that the product of their functioning is the very same organization that produces them." It is an organization of highly dynamic components whose effect is the production and maintenance of itself.

To characterize an organization that maintains itself while necessarily interacting with its environment, this research tradition employs two main notions, as introduced by Piaget (1967) and further elaborated by others. The first is *thermodynamic openness*: To exist far from equilibrium, that is, to contrast degradation or the thermodynamic tendency towards a homogeneous distribution (maximum disorder and minimum organization), a living system needs matter from the environment in the form of building blocks from which to produce its components, and energy to perform the activities required to maintain itself and interact with a changing environment. The second notion, which is specifically biological and aims to capture the distinctive feature of living systems, is *organizational closure*: A biological organization is characterized as a closed (i.e. circular) network of processes of production in which each component is produced by others in the network, such that the network maintains itself despite the continuous change at the level of its parts and the continuous interaction with the environment. The interplay between openness in the material dimension and closure in the organizational one ensures that matter and energy are admitted to the system from outside, but the processes that generate the work that continually remakes the organism are carried out by components produced by these very processes. According to this perspective, living systems need to be constantly at work to build and replace their components and extract from the environment the matter and energy necessary to run their internal processes. To use an expression by Bechtel, they are "endogenously active" (Bechtel, 2008) due to the thermodynamic nature of biological organization, which combines at its core endogenous activity with essential interaction with changing environments.

On this basis, this research tradition embraces a generative framework in which there is a mutual dependence between the components of an organism, such that the very existence of each component depends on its relationship with the others and with the system as a whole. Despite the common focus on relations, the organizational approach follows a different pathway from Rashevsky's Relational Biology discussed in the previous section. Instead of proceeding from the bottom up by identifying individual properties and functions and attempting to connect them, the organizational approach proceeds top-down. It recognizes the strong integration between mutually dependent components and processes in living organisms, which are capable of producing their parts and maintaining themselves, and it tries to understand which minimal organization is necessary to realize it. Once this organization is characterized, details can be filled in and it can be used to shed light on different biological phenomena in the context of the organism.[8]

The early organizational tradition is subject to two main limits. One is that these accounts are extremely abstract. One reason for this can be found in the heritage of Cybernetics and its emphasis on formal characterizations of organisms. Such formal analysis allows for multiple realizability: Different types of biological, physical, and mechanical components could realize the same abstract relations, such as feedback loops (see e.g. Varela & Maturana, 1972). A further reason is that advocates of the organizational or autonomy tradition sought to distinguish living organisms from other non-biological examples of far-from-equilibrium systems that were being advanced at the time in the physical sciences, such as dissipative structures (Glansdorff & Prigogine, 1971) like convection flows, hurricanes, whirlpools, and so on: thermodynamically open systems that realize stable patterns by consuming energy from the environment. While accepting that living systems are maintained in far-from-equilibrium conditions, and are themselves dissipative, the organizational framework of the sixties and seventies of the twentieth century emphasized that the distinctive character of biological systems was to be found in their organization rather than in their physical properties.

The other limit is that the notion of organizational closure was meant to provide general theoretical foundations for notions such as life and even cognition, interpreted as a biologically rooted phenomenon common to all organisms (Piaget, 1967; Maturana & Varela, 1980). In this perspective, closure plays the role of a general *explanans* from which a number of important implications about living systems could be developed. However, this early work puts considerably less effort into providing a detailed characterization of closure. For these early studies, the very organization of biological systems is not itself an *explanandum*; for that, causal relations and details about how they are realized need to be fleshed out.

During the last decades, work on biological organization has increasingly focused on addressing these limits. It has seen attempts to shift the focus from foregrounding the circularity of construction of biological system to emphasizing the need to also consider the thermodynamic requirements of maintaining an organized system far from equilibrium and to incorporate consideration of the material realization of living systems (Ruiz-Mirazo & Moreno, 2004). While doing so, it has developed conceptual tools to develop the notion of organizational closure and to characterize the causal relations it entails.

---

[8] In this view, organization is a key concept to understand biological systems and a theoretical hypothesis to guide research. According to Mossio et al. (2016) it can even be considered as a theoretical principle, that is, an a-priori overarching hypothesis that frames the intelligibility of biological objects.

Departing from the traditional characterization of organizational closure and inspired by the work of Pattee (1972) and Kauffman (2000), Moreno and Mossio (2015) and Montévil and Mossio (2015) emphasize the thermodynamics of organisms in a way that goes beyond the idea that organisms just need matter and energy: Organisms must constrain energy into the establishment of their own components. Organisms are far from equilibrium with their environments. Accordingly, they must perform work to build and repair their components. To do this work, they must procure energy from the environment and constrain it to construct and repair the components responsible for this activity as well as the other components and the physical structure that houses them. A pivotal role in accounting for this activity of living systems has been played by the notion of constraint. Constraints are defined as structures that act as local boundary conditions that enable specific processes and activities.[9] A constraint C can be defined as a material structure that harnesses a process P by reducing its degrees of freedom so that:

(1) at a time-scale characteristic of P, C is locally unaffected by P;
(2) at this time-scale C exerts a causal role on P, that is, there is some observable difference between free P, and P under the influence of C (Mossio et al., 2013).

Constraints exert a distinctive causal power, which consists in limiting the range of possible outcomes (degrees of freedom) of a process, thus making some possibilities more likely: They are both limiting and enabling. It is an asymmetric relationship inasmuch as a constraint is not part of the process it modifies, and it is stable during the time scale in which the process takes place. Through its activity, it canalizes a process towards outcomes that otherwise would be extremely improbable or practically impossible. An example of constraint is a pipe harnessing the flux of water from a pond so that it arrives to a tank located at a given distance across some hills and a valley: a process that would not occur, or not as efficiently, by diffusion alone. In this case, the constraint (i.e. the pipe) reduces the degrees of freedom of processes or collections of elements (the possible direction of movement of the molecules of water) in such a way that they exhibit specific behaviors (it enables water molecules to flow in the

---

[9] In classical mechanics, the term constraint stands for an asymmetrical relationship such as that holding between boundary conditions and dynamics. When the behavior of the system is underspecified, constraints constitute an alternative description that provides the missing specifications (normally by decreasing degrees of freedom). The notion of constraints has always escaped precise definition, besides the general acknowledgement of its role in providing additional specifications to dynamics that otherwise would be insufficiently (or incorrectly) described. The organizational approach, however, takes a different path, and characterizes constraints not as descriptive artifices but in terms of the causal role played by specific structures within a system.

same direction). This constrained behavior can be used to perform some coherent activity in the context of a system (such as water filling a tank or moving the wheel of a water mill). A typical example of a biological constraint is the activity of an enzyme, which catalyzes a reaction without being directly affected by it at the time scale in which the reaction takes place. What an enzyme does in its active site is to bind to substrate molecules and to hold them in place (i.e. restricting their freedom of movement in space so that their reactive sites can interact) in such a way that the processes of breaking or making of chemical bonds can take place more easily, thus lowering the activation energy required for the reaction between the substrates to take place.

Constraints harness processes, by specifying (at least part of) the conditions of existence of those processes. The notion of constraint so formulated allows us to distinguish between two orders of "causes" in natural systems: processes and those constraints that make those processes possible. The relevance of this definition lies in the fact that it allows us to describe not only the internal dynamics of a system but also to take into consideration the conditions of existence of these dynamics, in particular how in some cases they can be determined or affected by the activity of the system itself. An aspect of paramount importance is that although constraints are not changed during the interval during which they enable work to be done, they are themselves constructed over a distinct time frame. They are the result of production processes, which in turn require the presence of other constraints to be realized. By acting on those processes responsible for the production of other constraints, constraints are conditions of existence for them. The distinctive character of biological systems is that they are capable of generating from within some of the (internal) constraints that are necessary for their own functioning and for harnessing their internal dynamics (Moreno & Mossio, 2015). Some of these might be inherited from those constructed in a parent organism (Mossio & Pontarotti, 2022), but most are constructed by the organism itself during its lifespan.

This idea is captured by the notion of *closure of constraints* which has been introduced as a way to flesh out the causal relations implicit in the original notion of *organizational closure* (Montévil & Mossio, 2015). These causal relationships between constraints and processes are represented in Figure 2. In order for a biological system to maintain itself far from equilibrium with its environment, for each component C_4, that constrains a process in the system, at least one of the boundary conditions necessary for its maintenance and production are dependent on the activity of another constrain C_2 in the system, whose maintenance and existence directly or indirectly (through other constraints, e.g. C_3) depends, in turn, on C_4. By doing so, these constraints realize a distinctive circular causal regime by which they are organized in such a way that they are mutually dependent for their

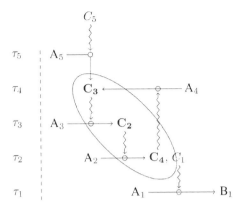

Figure 2 An abstract representation of closure of constraints (Montévil & Mossio, 2015, reproduced with permission from Elsevier). Straight arrows represent production processes. Wavy arrows represent the action of constraints C. A_{1-5} represents the material inputs of production processes, while B_1 represents a generic material output of the system. According to this diagram, constraint C_2 is a necessary condition for the production of constraint C_4 from the material substrate A_2. Constraint C_4 is a necessary condition for the production of constraint C_3 from A_4. C_3, in turn, is a necessary condition for the production of C_2 from A_3. So organized, the three constraints C_2, C_3, and C_4 form a closed loop in which they are mutually dependent for their existence.

production and maintenance, and collectively contribute to the maintenance of the conditions in which the whole network can persist. In virtue of realizing closure of constraints, a living system is able to maintain its dynamical organization despite the constant transformations and turnover at the level of components.

This framework is characterized by a distinctive approach to understanding and explaining biological phenomena. It is primarily focused on current biological systems, such as organisms, rather than historical phenomena such as the evolution of lineages. It aims to explain the maintenance of living systems by studying their physiology and behavior in order to understand how they are or can be maintained here and now. In a living system, understood in terms of a causal regime of closure of constraints, a multiplicity of constraints contributes in different ways to the maintenance of their organization. To provide an explanation of a given phenomenon, one would need to identify the processes involved and the different constraints that make them possible, and how both processes and constraints contribute to the maintenance of the system that harbors them.[10] Let us think, for example, of

---

[10] Cusimano and Sterner (2020) question the possibility of univocally operationalizing constraints and consequently closure of constraints. They call for more examples to be analyzed to show

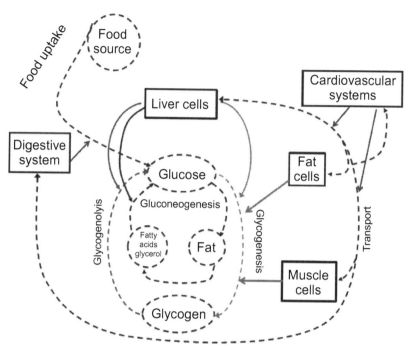

Figure 3 General representation of glucose uptake, distribution, and transformation. Processes are represented by dashed arrows, metabolic substrates by dashed circles, constraints by rectangular boxes and their activities by full arrows. The digestive system includes the set of constraints responsible for the uptake of food, including glucose, which is then distributed throughout the body by another set of constraints, the cardiovascular system. Transporters and enzymes in liver, fat, and muscle cells are the constraints responsible for glucose uptake and metabolism (glycolysis, glycogenolysis, and gluconeogenesis). All these constraints are produced and maintained by the system. Figure reprinted from Bich et al. (2020) under Creative Commons License (CC BY-SA 4.0).

the phenomenon of glucose uptake and transformation through the digestive system in mammals (Figure 3, see Bich et al., 2020 for more details). One can identify at least seven processes with the relative constraints acting on them: (1) *food uptake*, constrained by the digestive system (the constraints involved are the digestive tube, the digestive enzymes, and the epithelial cells that absorb glucose in the intestine); (2) *glucose distribution* within the system through the bloodstream, constrained by the vascular system; (3) *glucose uptake* by cells of different tissues,

---

otherwise. In their view, the attribution of closure would depend on the explanatory problem addressed.

constrained by glucose transporters in the cell membrane; (4) *intracellular glycolysis*, the breaking down of glucose molecules into pyruvate as part of the process of production of ATP,[11] a process constrained by intracellular enzymes; (5) *glycogenesis*, which consists of the transformation of glucose into glycogen for storage, constrained mainly by enzymes in liver cells, striated muscles cells, and cells of the white adipose tissue; (6) *glycogenolysis*, the transformation of stored glycogen into glucose, constrained by enzymes in all cells that store glycogen; and (7) *gluconeogenesis*, constrained by enzymes in liver cells, which produce glucose anew starting from amino acids, lipids, pyruvate, and lactate. Closure is realized by the fact that each part acting as a constraint is also the product of metabolic biosynthetic processes taking place within the system, and glucose is used as a source of energy for running the metabolic processes of the system. As a result of these activities, the system maintains itself.

The notion of closure of constraints constitutes a refined version of organizational closure in which different types of entities (constraints and processes) and causal relations are made explicit. It focuses on the distinctive capability of living systems to contribute to their own conditions of existence. It establishes a generative dependence between components through a closed topology of transformation processes in which internally produced components constitute a subset of the conditions of existence for those processes. However, this circularity at the level of constraints should not be confused with any cycle of activities at the level of processes. Cycles are captured by a different circularity that is also known as *closure of processes* or *operational closure*, which stands for the recursion between the operations of the components of a system: a closed network of operations in which all the actions of the components have an effect inside the system. To realize closure of constraints, and therefore a self-maintaining organization, what is important is not only that the results of the activities of parts remain within the system, but that for any component its production process can be traced within the system. The circularity realized by closure of constraints encompasses not only the activities of the components but their conditions of existence, provided by their participation in the organized system they continuously realize. While the notion of cycle, or operational closure, says nothing about the origin of the components, organizational closure points to their internal generation as well as to the properties they need to satisfy in order to contribute to self-production, that is, to be able to participate in processes of production – transformation and degradation – of other components. This is a feature that is not shared by other circular networks such as abiotic water cycles or self-maintaining systems such as dissipative structures

---

[11] The fundamental energy molecule used to power cellular activities.

like hurricanes and whirlwinds (see Mossio & Bich, 2017). These latter do not produce their own components and do not determine the condition of existence of their processes, but are mostly and largely determined by external boundary conditions, and emerge spontaneously under appropriate environmental conditions.[12]

In the introduction I argued that to understand living organisms and their capability of maintaining themselves despite the fragility of their components, one needs to take into account two main closely interconnected features of biological systems: self-production and self-regulation. In this section, I have shown how self-production is accounted for in terms of organization by the notion of closure of constraints. In the next section, I will extend this framework and complete the theoretical picture by turning on self-regulation.

4 Reinterpreting Closure: From Basic Self-Maintenance to Regulatory Control

This section addresses some of the limits of the notion of closure of constraint. It discusses how the conceptual core of the organizational framework and the notion of biological self-maintenance can be developed and improved by taking into consideration not only self-production but also self-regulation as the two fundamentally intertwined properties that are necessary to characterize biological systems. While the first is captured by the notion of closure of constraints, the second is accounted for by the notion of regulatory control. ·

As mentioned in the introductory section, a distinctive feature of biological organisms is that to be alive, they need to engage in a variety of activities that allow them to keep living. They do not just replace and repair their parts, but also modify themselves and what they (and their parts) do based on their internal physiological state and environmental conditions. However, current notions of closure and organization have been focusing primarily on the mutual dependence between functional components of biological systems (characterized as constraints) for their production and repair, considered as the core foundation of the theoretical

---

[12] Equating closure of constraints and cycles means overlooking the generative dimension and the contribution to the conditions of existence of a system that characterize closure of constraints. This may lead to putting together phenomena that are qualitatively different from an organizational point of view. An example of this conceptual confusion can be found in Garson's discussion of panic disorders as cases of self-maintaining organizations subject to closure (Garson, 2017). He exploits such cases to criticize the organizational framework as too liberal, insofar as it would include in a regime of closure phenomena that do not contribute to the maintenance of the system. However, the example discussed is a case of cycle, more precisely of a behavior that reinforces itself. Like in the case of an abiotic cycle, this self-reinforcing behavior indeed exhibits circularity and feeds into itself. But it does so at the level of operations or processes, not of the constraints that generate those operations and processes, which are instead extrinsic to the phenomenon. Therefore, it does not realize closure.

framework (Montévil & Mossio, 2015). By doing so, this research line has tended to assume that what characterizes the core organization of biological systems is the causal regime of production of components (closure) which achieves self-maintenance based on productive relationships alone. The causal regime of closure has been understood as inherently stable, and the activity of its parts characterized by regularity when not affected by potentially disruptive environmental perturbations that cannot be compensated for by building new parts to replace those damaged (Mossio et al., 2016).[13] The implicit assumption underlying this idea is that under invariant and not threatening environmental conditions, closure is sufficient to account for biological self-maintenance and to capture the distinctive features of biological organizations. The idea of regulation is considered as an additional, not definitory, feature of biological organizations: a capacity employed only in cases in which the system is subject to strong perturbations that risk endangering its viability. I will argue that the role of regulatory control in biological systems is instead deeper and concerns every activity carried out by biological systems, not only those related to response to perturbations. We cannot think of closure without also considering regulation.[14]

The notion of closure of constraints has the merit of having provided a theoretical characterization of the dimension of self-production of biological systems and its underlying causal regime, compatible with their thermodynamic requirements (Moreno & Mossio, 2015). In such a way it has overcome some of the shortcomings of previous accounts of biological organization such as the theory of autopoiesis, which had reached an impasse for several decades, notably due to their lack of causal details and the detachment from material considerations (see also Bich & Bechtel, 2021, 2022a). However, by focusing on production, repair, and replacement of components to characterize the causal regime of biological systems, the basic notion of closure of constraints is still too narrow to capture the distinctive features of biological organizations and provide a theoretical understanding of them. This is due to three types of problems, which concern, specifically, its biological grounding, the capability to account for the integration between components, and for change (adaptive, physiological, developmental, etc.).

---

[13] "Organization enables the maintenance of constitutive constraints, beyond their characteristic time scales, through the continuous reestablishment of their mutual dependences. In this respect, one might describe the overall stability of closure as the result of a kind of 'organizational inertia'. Because of the network of mutual dependencies, biological organization tends to remove variations affecting local constraints and to regenerate them in a fundamentally unaltered form" (Mossio et al., 2016: 31–32).

[14] As argued by Cornish-Bowden and Cardenas regarding different accounts of organizational closure: "All of these incorporate the idea of circularity to some extent, but all of them fail to take account of mechanisms of metabolic regulation, which we regard as crucial if an organism is to avoid collapsing into a mass of unregulated reactions" (Cornish-Bowden & Cardenas, 2020: 1).

With regards to biological grounding, the notion of closure of constraints selects from the set of relations realized in biological systems the generative ones involved in the production of components. This operation allows one to address and characterize with clarity the mutual dependence between production process and those constraints responsible for them. However, this comes at the price of abstracting away other essential relations. In actual biological systems, the basic constraints involved in a regime of closure are not always functioning, or functioning whenever their substrates and energy are available. Their activities are constantly controlled: inhibited, activated, and modulated. Let us think of some basic biological activities. The production of ATP from glucose is not carried out constantly, but only when its level is low, and energy is needed by the cell. Cells do not divide continuously, but they engage in division only at some given moments. Neurons generate action potentials, but appropriate stimuli either increase or decrease the rate of firing. Even a fundamental activity such as protein synthesis, responsible for the production of those constraints (such as enzymes) participating in the core regime of closure, is not carried out all the time and for all proteins. It is inhibited or activated on the basis of the needs of the cell. Just as a cell cannot carry out all possible activities continuously and simultaneously, it does not synthesize all its possible proteins at the same time and all the time, due to spatial and energetic limitations. These examples show that to maintain itself, an organism needs to continuously modulate and coordinate the activities of its basic constraints that directly harness thermodynamic processes, in such a way that they can realize a viable regime of closure. When looking at each of the constraints involved in closure, one should consider that whether, when and how they act on processes, is constantly subject to other types of organizational conditions not captured in the abstract diagrams of closure shown in Figures 2 and 3.

Let us consider the second problem: integration. Closure emphasizes the mutual dependence between components for their production but does not account for how their activities are also mutually dependent so that components are integrated into a system that maintains itself as a cohesive whole. In living systems, different parts or groups of parts provide different and specific contributions to the functioning and maintenance of the system. Harboring components capable of playing different tasks such as catalysis, transport, compartmentalization, signaling, DNA transcription, translation, protein synthesis, and so on, is a fundamental requirement for division of labor. However, besides producing all these components and thus ensuring their presence within the system, a cohesive integration between these different tasks is only achieved when those different activities are orchestrated so that they collectively contribute to the maintenance of the system. Only those activities needed in the current situation need to be carried out. Moreover, some parts or subsystems may work differently and with different requirements, which are not always compatible. One example is photosynthesis and nitrogen fixation in cyanobacterium *Synechococcus* discussed in the introduction: two mutually exclusive processes that need to be carried out at different times. In other cases, specific activities need to be carried out only when others have already been completed or some specific requirements are satisfied. For this to happen, the components' activities need to be modulated in such a way that each operates when needed and in a way that is compatible with the state of the system and the activities of the other components while avoiding potential conflicts.

Let us move to the third problem: change. Organization theorists have not denied that there is variability and change in living organisms, but while a lot of effort has been put into emphasizing the continuity of a biological organization through a life cycle (Di Frisco & Mossio, 2020), change has been often screened off from their accounts as extrinsic to a biological organization and not strictly required for it to function. Some proponents of the organizational view have even argued that organization and variation should be considered as two distinct theoretical principles (Montévil et al., 2016; Mossio et al., 2016). In this view, the biological organization that realizes closure is inherently stable, while variation is something that happens to this organization during ontogeny and evolution (through randomness, perturbations, mutations, etc.).[15] Variation is regarded as a source of noise: external to a biological organization and not required (or employed) for its viable functioning. This is a problem for several reasons. As argued by Bich and Bechtel (2022b), regularity and stability in the activity of components are exceptions within living organisms. A living system coordinates the activities of its components, modulates internal processes, and responds adaptively to environmental variations. It can undergo drastic modification of its basic organization such as during development (Bich & Skillings, 2023). The activity of each basic constraint is continuously modulated according to the needs of the organization, starting from those basic constraints involved in transcription, translation, and protein synthesis, so that each activity is performed in ways appropriate to the circumstances the system faces and its internal state. Change, often radical, is at the core of the functioning of biological systems, and accounts of biological organization need to address it. However, as argued by Bich et al. (2016) closure alone would account only for a very limited type of change, understood in terms of dynamic stability, a passive network property: The basic

---

[15] Montevil et al. (2016) include contextuality among the sources of variation. However, as explained in this section, closure alone does not exhibit this property as it does not account for the system's sensitivity to the context and capacity to modify itself accordingly.

regime of closure would simply "absorb" as a network the effects of a limited set of perturbations or internal variations (such as lack or increase of supply, damage to some components, etc.). It would do so by compensating for these perturbations through internal reciprocal adjustments between tightly coupled processes (e.g. through increased or decreased production of components to replace damaged ones, increased rates of processes, variation in the amount of supply metabolites consumed, etc.), while the whole dynamic is maintained in the initial attractor, or it is pushed by the perturbation into a new stable attractor. The focus on repair and replacement of parts, for example, emphasizes restoring the organism to its stable condition. Dynamic stability cannot account for how at different times, and depending on its internal state, that of the environment and the availability of food, a living system modifies itself by modulating and fine-tuning its own activities and also undergoes radical changes. This is especially relevant if one considers that the system continuously shifts between different types of metabolism enabled by distinct sets of enzymes, between a regime of cell growth and one of cell division, between different directions of movement to look for nutrients or avoid predators, and so on.

In sum, the notion of closure of constraints has emphasized how the parts of a living system are produced, transformed, and repaired from within the system. However, to remain viable, both to carry out those basic physiological activities required to realize closure when and how they are needed, and to face changing environments, biological organizations must also behave adaptively, changing what activities they perform in ways appropriate to the circumstances they face. Only by deploying such adaptive capacities can organisms integrate the activities of their components and counteract potentially destabilizing interactions with the environment. In line with some insights anticipated by Piaget (1967), Di Paolo (2005) and Bitbol and Luisi (2004) emphasized the importance of developing the organizational framework, and specifically the notion of autopoiesis, in this direction. To do so advocates of the organizational framework have introduced into their account and developed the notion of regulatory control, characterized as an activity carried out by a special type of constraints: control constraints (Bich et al., 2016).

What is control? Control is generally understood in biology as the capability to actively modify the dynamics of a system towards certain states in a given situation (Rosen, 1970). Metabolic control, for example, is characterized as a modification of the state of metabolism in response to signals (Fell, 1997). Control implies an asymmetric interaction: There is a controller that acts upon a controlled process, component, or subsystem. A system able to control itself, such as a biological one, should be able to employ different control components to modify its internal processes and the activities of its other components depending on internal and external conditions. Within the organizational frame-work, accounting for this kind of relation requires introducing a special type of constraint. Most constraints are realized by structures that statically reduce the degrees of freedom of the process they canalize. It is the case of a pipe in artificial systems, of a semipermeable membrane or a simple enzyme in a biological system. This may be sufficient to enable and harness a process. Control, however, implies something more, that is, the capability of modulating and coordinating the activities of the components of a system towards a certain behavior or goal state. This cannot be achieved by means of static structural constraints. As pointed out by early work by Howard Pattee (1972), control requires a dynamic constraint that can actively select between different possible outcomes or activities available in the process or component on which it operates and modifies. This can be achieved, for example, when a constraint enables or inhibits a process in the presence of signal molecules or specific conditions in its surroundings. By operating in this way, control constraints do not just reduce degrees of freedom once and for all, for example by restricting the flow of fluid in one specific direction. Instead, they are sensitive to the state of the system or the environment, and they modulate the controlled process or the behavior of other constraints accordingly (Bich et al., 2016; Winning & Bechtel, 2018).[16]

Control constraints are a special type of constraint that are dynamic and do not operate on production or repair processes but on the activities of other constraints: They are second-order constraints. In biological systems, control constraints play a regulatory role as they do not just modify the activities of other constraints on the basis of what they sense, but in doing so they contribute to the maintenance of the organisms that produce and maintain those very constraints. Let us consider a simple case of biological control protein: a kinase protein. This protein is produced within the system, but instead of contributing directly to the generation of other constraints in the system (like metabolic enzymes and other basic constraints involved in closure of constraints do), it phosphorylates other proteins (enzymes) thus modifying their conformation and their activities (inhibiting, activating, modulating them). However, a kinase does not do that every time it encounters a given enzyme, but only under specific conditions. It changes its activation status on the basis of the interaction with a ligand or a signal molecule at a different site than the effector site (the one where it exerts its constraining activity on enzymes) and modifies the activity of other constraints based on such interaction.

---

[16] See Section 7 for more details on Winning and Bechtel's proposal.

Within the organizational framework, regulatory control entails an architecture of constraints (Figure 4) that satisfies four main requirements: (1) some constraints Rs are higher order because they modulate the activity of other constraints instead of directly channeling metabolic processes (as first-order constraints Cs described by closure do); (2) these regulatory control constraints Rs are themselves made within the system through the activities of other constraints Cs, hence subject to closure (otherwise the source of control would be extrinsic to the system); (3) they must be sensitive to variations and capable of performing different activities depending on what they sense;[17] and (4) by modifying the operations carried out by other constraints, these higher-order constraints must contribute to the maintenance of the system.

To better illustrate the idea, let us consider a biological example of regulatory control that induces changes in how metabolism is carried out depending on the presence or absence of specific metabolites. Bacteria need the amino acid tryptophan for their metabolism. They take this amino acid from the environment, but they are also able to start producing it when it is not available from external sources. They can modulate the production of tryptophan through the regulatory control of the transcription step of the synthesis of the enzymes necessary to synthesize the amino acid. The genes encoding for the five enzymes that contribute to the production of tryptophan (the first-order constraints C involved in the regime of closure) are grouped together into one operon. A repressor protein (the regulator R) exerts regulatory control upon the promoter of the operon. Two molecules of this amino acid act as the signals that are necessary to activate the repressor protein. In the presence of tryptophan, the repressor protein interacts with two of these molecules, it is activated and binds to the promoter of the operon. By doing so, it represses the synthesis of the enzymes responsible for the metabolism of tryptophan and blocks the endogenous production of this amino acid. In the absence of tryptophan, instead, the repressor protein is in an inhibited state and does not bind to the promoter region of the operon. When the promoter of the operon is unbound, the transcription of the operon can start and the cell can synthesize the enzymes responsible for the production of the amino acid, which can then be used in biosynthetic pathways within the bacterial cell.

---

[17] The operation of a control constraint on other constraints depends on the conditions it senses. This entails that the activity of the components used in regulatory control are not totally determined by the processes that produce them, although their presence in the system depends on those. They are operationally independent, or "dynamically decoupled," from what they control (Bich et al., 2016), in the sense that they exhibit some degrees of freedom that are not specified by the dynamics of the controlled constraints. Otherwise, they would be fully constrained by the dynamics of metabolism and not free to respond to the conditions they sense and act upon them. Such a local operational independence allows regulatory subsystems to modulate other constraints in a relatively autonomous way.

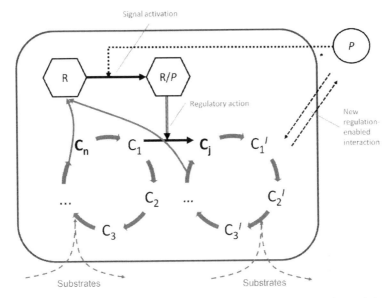

Figure 4 General relational diagram of regulatory control as the activity of second (or higher)-order constraints (Bich et al., 2016, reproduced with permission from Springer Nature). Cs are constraints involved in the basic regime of closure of constraints; Rs are regulatory control constraints; P is an environmental perturbation. Rs are sensitive to P and modify the activities of Cs accordingly. Gray lines represent production processes. Black lines represent regulatory processes. Full arrows represent intra-system processes, dotted arrows signal interactions that trigger the activation of Rs, and dashed arrows interactive processes with the environment.[18]

Regulatory control, as employed in this case, is what allows biological systems to modulate the activities of their components coherently with the internal state of the organism and that of the environment. It is a fundamental requirement for the realization and functioning of a causal regime of closure as much as closure is for the production of regulatory constraints. For closure to be realized and to be viable, the *activity* of each constraint C depends on the operations of at least one regulatory constraint R, which in turn depends on C for its *existence*. As argued earlier, the need for regulation arises not just as a response to environmental perturbations, but also as a result of the fact that living systems possess multiple capacities resulting from the constraints they build within themselves. In order for living systems to succeed in building, repairing, and reproducing themselves,

---

[18] For explanatory purposes, the diagram describes regulation in the context of interaction with a changing environment represented by P, but it can be applied to regulatory phenomena based on the detection of internal states.

they need to coordinate these capacities by regulating their activities so that they are performed when and how they are required to accomplish these ends. This provides a richer view of self-maintenance beyond self-production: Due to regulatory control, organisms can select activities on the basis of what they sense and in so doing they contribute to their own maintenance. By taking into account both closure and regulation, one can characterize a biological organization as consisting of different components integrated into a cohesive unit. These components are related in such a way that they depend on one another for their own production, maintenance, and also activity so that they collectively contribute to maintaining the organization that harbors them.[19]

Including regulatory control in the organizational framework also provides richer, more detailed and biologically grounded explanations of biological phenomena. Let us go back to the example of glucose metabolism discussed in the previous section and described in Figure 3. From the point of view of closure, the main processes and constraints considered are those that uptake, distribute, and consume glucose. An equally important aspect is how and when glucose is used, transported inside cells, made available for metabolism or stored. These activities depend on the energetic needs of the organisms for movement and metabolism, and need to prevent high concentrations of glucose in the bloodstream after feeding. To provide a more comprehensive explanation of this phenomenon from an organizational perspective, one needs to consider, besides basic processes and constraints, also the regulatory control constraints involved and how they operate on the other constraints to maintain the system: for example, by activating or inhibiting them or selecting between different processes to be carried out under different conditions. In the example of glucose regulation, the main sources of control constraints are pancreatic alpha and beta cells (Figure 5, B). By sensing their intracellular levels of ATP (which depend indirectly on the presence and concentration of glucose in the blood), they release hormones. One is insulin, which (released by beta cells) directly modulates glucose transport into cells and the transformation of glucose into glycogen

---

[19] It is important to point out that regulatory constraints do not usually act individually on distinct first-order constraints. Each biological activity is controlled by different constraints, so that the system can modulate its activities by taking into consideration multiple internal and external conditions, such as for example the availability of energy, the presence of nutrients, predators, and toxins in the environment, the alternance of daylight and darkness, and so on. Moreover, regulatory constraints can be controlled in turn by other regulatory constraints in the system and there is ongoing crosstalk between them. A further step in characterizing biological organizations is to address how regulatory constraints interact and are themselves integrated. See Bechtel and Bich (2021) and Bich and Bechtel (2022b) for a general discussion of this dimension of biological organizations and Bich and Bechtel (2022a) and Bechtel and Bich (2023) for a detailed analysis of two specific case studies: integrated regulation in the bacteria *E. coli* and in the multicellular worm *C. elegans*, respectively.

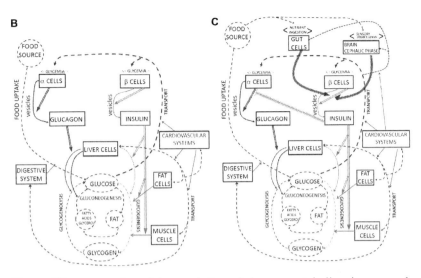

Figure 5 Representation of the regulation of glucose metabolism in mammals (Bich et al., 2020). The basic processes and constraints involved in glucose metabolism appear as described in Figure 3. **B.** Second-order regulatory constraints are represented by those boxes whose activities are represented by double arrows. The conditions to which they are sensitive are represented by <Xs>above the pertinent boxes. Regulatory constraints such as insulin and glucagon modify glucose transport into the cell and intracellular glucose metabolism. **C.** Higher-order regulatory constraints, such as the nervous system and gut cells, operate on second-order constraints. Their activities are represented by triple arrows. Figure reprinted from Bich et al. (2020) under Creative Commons License (CC BY-SA 4.0).

to be stored in liver cells. The other is glucagon, released by alpha cells, which activates the production of glucose from glycogen stored in the liver. These activities are selected depending on the level of glucose in the bloodstream (high or low respectively) and the energetic needs of the organism. In turn (Figure 5, C), the secretive activities of pancreatic beta cells are controlled by further higher-order control constraints in the system. These include the nervous system and gut cells, which start stimulating the release of insulin before the increase in glucose levels happens, when the mammal sees the food and the food enters the digestive system, to anticipate and counteract more quickly the rise in glucose concentration.

After having introduced and discussed the conceptual foundations of the organizational framework and illustrated them through examples, in the next two sections I discuss how this framework has been applied in philosophy and biology.

5 Naturalizing Biological Teleology and Functions

The previous two sections have discussed the conceptual basis of the organizational framework: the intertwined notions of closure and regulation. We can now move to address how this framework has been applied to ground and naturalize two central notions in the philosophy of biology: teleology (Mossio & Bich, 2017) and function (Mossio et al., 2009; see also McLaughlin, 2001 and Christensen & Bickhard, 2002).[20] They represent two ways to account for how living systems can be characterized as having goals. Teleology aims to explain why and how goals can be ascribed to biological systems as wholes. For example, let us think of nutrition. A living system as a whole can be said to have the goal of procuring and absorbing the nutrients it needs to survive. Nutrition requires a living system to seek food in its environment, move to catch it, then to ingest and digest it, and to process the resulting nutrients to use them as building blocks and energy sources or to store them, while expelling waste. Functions instead are ascribed to parts or specific traits of those purposive systems. A classic example is an organ such as the heart, whose function as part of a living system can be said to be to pump blood around the body through the vascular system. The organizational framework naturalizes the notions of teleology and function in a different way than most other accounts, by looking at the current organization of a biological system, instead of its evolutionary history.

5.1 Organization and Teleology

A challenge faced by biology is to make sense of those biological phenomena that take place in a way that is, or appears to be, oriented towards goals, to understand what is distinctive of them and how they differ from similar phenomena occurring in purely physical, chemical, and mechanical systems.[21] Those latter consist of processes that converge to a specific end-state (or process) from a range of initial conditions, such as a marble falling in a bowl, or a chemical system that goes back to equilibrium after having been displaced from it. They are described as oriented towards an end-state, and they can be usually described dynamically in terms of attractors.

Tending towards an end-state, however, is different from having goals and acting in order to achieve them. When we say that an animal is seeking food, we seem to be saying more than that it is settling into an attractor. Having and pursuing goals is what we usually attribute to living organisms based on our

---

[20] These are two of the contributions of the organizational framework that have had more philosophical impact, especially the account of biological functions.

[21] For a more detailed discussion of these ideas see for example Mossio and Bich (2017) and Dresow and Love (2023).

everyday experiences, when we observe how they act in such a way as to persist in their changing and often challenging environments: from looking for food to escaping predators. Biology, therefore, seems to harbor phenomena that are goal-oriented in a more fundamental sense, when compared to the physico-chemical domain. This idea of goals is captured by the notion of *teleology*, that is, the explanation of phenomena by reference to the purpose they serve. Teleological vocabulary is widespread in biology, for example, when talking of several important notions such as the function of parts, or phenomena such as physiological regulation, behavior, and so on. However, teleological phenomena are not exclusive to biology. Other classes of systems, such as artifacts, can be described as teleological. We ascribe goals to artifacts as tools, from without: They have goals for a designer or for a user. Their goals are therefore extrinsic. When we say that biological systems pursue goals, we are not doing it for the same reasons we ascribe goals to artifacts. We do not usually ascribe goals to a living system in terms of what we can do with it, unless we are using it as a tool (e.g. when we use yeast to leaven bread and ferment alcoholic beverages). What is different in the case of a living system is that goals play a role within the system itself: We ascribe goals to a living system because what the system does has some importance to the system itself. In this view, biological goals are intrinsic.

The challenges of addressing biological teleology are multiple. One needs to account for purposes and goals in a way that is scientifically grounded, by providing naturalized explanations. These explanations can be important in order to understand why living systems behave in some ways and not others, and to ground several notions, starting with functions. They also need to capture the distinctive intrinsic teleological dimension of living systems, compared to the extrinsic one of artifacts and to the directedness exhibited by some physical and chemical systems.

Biological teleology aims to explain the presence of a system in terms of what it does. According to advocates of the organizational framework, accounts of biological teleology such as the evolutionary and the organizational ones share a common naturalization strategy, which relates teleology to the contribution to the conditions of existence of a system: They both look for a circular causal regime such that the conditions of existence of a biological entity can be said – in a scientifically acceptable way – to depend on its own effects (Mossio & Bich, 2017). In both cases, biological teleology is naturalized by identifying the *telos* with the conditions of existence of the relevant system. While sharing a common strategy, evolutionary, and organizational accounts differ with respect to the regime responsible for the realization of this causal circularity and what is the system that realizes it.

The organizational framework focuses on current systems as the grounds for teleology and biological organization as the relevant causal regime in terms of which to naturalize teleology. This constitutes a Kantian approach to teleology, which develops Kant's idea, provided in the Critique of Judgement (1790/1987), that organisms can be characterized teleologically as "natural purposes," that is, systems in which the components exist for the whole they generate and the whole exists for the components it produces and maintains.[22] Specifically, the organizational framework focuses on how individual organisms maintain themselves and survive in their environment. To address teleology, it appeals to the relationship between conditions of existence of a biological entity and its own activity. By doing so, it aims to establish a connection between organization and teleology through the concept of self-determination (Mossio & Bich, 2017).

The theoretical starting point for understanding this relationship is the idea of closure of constraints, analyzed in Section 3, according to which the components of a biological system are mutually dependent insofar as they act as constraints for the processes responsible for the production and maintenance of other components in the system, on which in turn, they depend. One of the features of closure is that by acting on those processes responsible for the production of other constraints, constraints are conditions of existence for other constraints in the systems. In doing so, each constraint contributes to the maintenance of (some of) the conditions under which the whole network can exist. As a result, the whole organization of constraints achieves self-determination as self-constraint: a regime in which the conditions of existence of the constitutive constraints are mutually determined within and by the organization itself.

This causal regime can ground teleology because it establishes a circular relationship between the existence and activity of a living system. According to this view, a living system is what it does – it is a cause and effect of itself. Inasmuch as the effects of the activity of living systems contribute to establishing and maintaining their own conditions of existence and those of their parts, it can be said that the existence of the system and its parts depends on their effects. This allows organizational theorists to ground teleology in an organization that realizes a regime of closure of constraints, and to identify the intrinsic goal (*telos*) of a living organism with the maintenance of the conditions of existence on which the organization exerts a causal influence.

---

[22] Kauffman (2000) and Weber and Varela (2002) are among the first to underline this Kantian legacy. Gambarotto and Nahas (2022) distinguish two different types of Kantian approaches to biological teleology: heuristic and naturalistic. The first considers Kant's teleology as a heuristic tool for producing explanations of biological phenomena. The second sees in Kant's idea of natural purposes a new way to think about biological systems that should be developed by naturalizing teleology and turning it into a legitimate scientific concept. The organizational account of teleology would belong to the second type of Kantian approach.

This account can address the challenges to biological teleology mentioned at the beginning of this section. It can differentiate between the intrinsic teleology of biological systems and the extrinsic teleology of artifacts. Biological teleology is intrinsic because the circular relation between existence and activity takes place *within* the system considered. In artifacts, instead, the telos is distinct from the conditions of existence: The goal of a tool is not to maintain itself, although it has something to do with its existence since it is designed for a certain use. In this view, biological teleology can also be distinguished from the directionality exhibited, among others, by physical systems. Whereas teleology depends on a circularity between existence and activity, directionality consists in the convergence to an end-state and can be relevantly captured in terms of equifinality. It is an effect of a given causal regime, not also a cause.[23]

Evolutionary accounts of biological teleology (e.g. Millikan, 1989; Neander, 1991) – which are the most used in the philosophy of biology – take instead the lineage as the grounds of teleology, and natural selection as the relevant causal regime. Selection allows one to consider the history of organisms as teleological, insofar as the existence of a type of trait can be explained by the fact that the ancestors of the organisms carrying the trait survived due to having that trait. These accounts characterize teleology etiologically, in terms of contributions of traits to the survival of the ancestors of current organisms, so that biological goals are characterized in terms of adaptation by natural selection (inasmuch as they con-tribute to maintain the lineage). Advocates of the organizational perspective criticize evolutionary accounts by arguing that they fall into a form of "epipheno-menalism" (Christensen & Bickhard, 2002; Mossio et al., 2009; Mossio & Bich, 2017) in that they implicitly presuppose the existence of individual organisms able to survive and reproduce in their environment, that is, on individual adaptive organizations. Moreover, while maintaining themselves, organisms may pursue ends that do not relate to past selection. Based on this criticism, the teleological dimension of living organisms might not be considered as the result of natural selection but rather as its condition (Gambarotto, 2023).[24]

---

[23] This is another important distinction between the organizational framework and the cybernetic approach discussed in Section 2. Cyberneticians, while attempting to identify phenomena common to artificial and living systems, identify teleology with directionality, and the telos of a subsystem with its end-state (Rosenblueth et al., 1943). They do so by focusing on individual mechanisms or simple organizational motifs. However, by ignoring the relationship between activity and existence of a system and the self-maintaining nature of biological organizations, they cannot distinguish extrinsic from intrinsic teleology, that is, between cases in which a mechanism or motif is built and employed by a designer/user or by the system itself (see Jonas, 1953; Mossio & Bich, 2017; Sachs, 2023).

[24] This does not mean that the organizational framework is pursuing a better or more fundamental approach. This type of discussion would just assume the form of an endless "egg or chicken came first" debate. Organizational and evolutionary approaches should be seen instead as complementary.

Evolutionary accounts focus on functions and traits. They look outside organisms rather than inside of them to ground teleology, and they do so in terms of natural selection. The organizational framework, instead, characterizes biological systems as inherently teleological, which means that their own activity is, in a fundamental sense, first and foremost oriented towards an end. The organization of a living system is an intrinsically teleological causal regime where the conditions of existence on which the organization exerts a causal influence are the goal (telos) of the system. A distinctive feature and virtue of this organism-centered view is indeed its focus on the system as a whole, rather than just its parts or traits, and its characterization as intrinsically oriented towards an end: "teleology is not restricted to biological functions but understood as the intrinsic goal-directedness of whole organisms" (Nahas & Sachs, 2023: 2). By doing so, the organizational account provides the framework to discuss teleology more generally as a feature of biological systems rather than their traits or parts only.

The organizational approach, however, it is not the only non-evolutionary approach to biological teleology focused on organisms. Other non-evolutionary approaches include the so-called "behavioral approaches" (Nahas & Sachs, 2023). These assume teleology at the outset, and they use it to describe how organisms interact with their environments. One example is represented by the enactive approach, which follows a Hegelian rather than Kantian approach (see Gambarotto & Mossio, 2024): It treats organisms as purposeful systems by assuming they have a teleological organization, and focuses on describing their behaviors. Another example is constituted by Denis Walsh's approach, which also assumes that organisms are teleological, and addresses evolutionary processes in terms of goal-directed agents (Walsh, 2015). The main difference between these approaches and the organizational one is that in them teleology plays only the role of *explanans* and not also of *explanandum*. Their focus is not on how self-maintenance is achieved and they do not aim to naturalize *strictu sensu* teleology, but they employ the notion to explain and naturalize other phenomena.

One of the features, and perhaps a limitation, of the organizational account of teleology, which characterizes it in terms of contribution to establishing and maintaining the conditions of existence of the system (i.e. idea that "the system is what it does"), is that it is very minimal. The core idea is that the system and its parts do what they do, or they and the system would not exist. In a regime of basic closure (production of components), the effects of the activity of the system are teleological in a minimal sense as they contribute to establishing and maintaining its own conditions of existence. The basic constraints involved in closure realize this regime. They do what they do, and in so doing they contribute to the maintenance of the system. Developing a minimalist account is useful in order to provide a basic philosophical and theoretical grounding for the notion of teleology, a minimal common starting point from which to consider a system as teleological. However, this may constitute a limit if the minimal account is not employed as a stepstone to building a richer view that can precisely account for more fundamental features of biological systems and a wider range of phenomena. Living systems are teleological not only because their parts operate and, as an effect, contribute to maintaining the system. They also perform their activities when and in such a way as to maintain the system. A teleological regime is not just realized or not depending on whether the components of a system are working. It can also be realized in different ways depending on the circumstances. Organisms, while maintaining themselves, select between different available courses of action on the basis of their needs and environmental conditions. This more active feature of biological systems is not explicitly captured by the minimal notion of organizational teleology developed in terms of self-determination by Mossio and Bich (2017). The reason for this lies in the fact that this notion is grounded in the notion of closure, which focuses on self-production. Therefore, the minimal notion of organizational teleology does not account for the variability of the behaviors of parts, how they are integrated and orchestrated, and how they allow the system to change. As a consequence, it cannot distinguish between minimal and active purposefulness.

To better capture the distinctive teleological dimension of biological organizations, one needs to consider how organisms not only establish but actively exert a control over the way they contribute to their own conditions of existence (i.e. over the activity of basic productive constraints). As with regards to closure, one way to enrich the organizational account of the teleology and to include these fundamental purposeful activities is to take into account regulatory control. As shown in Section 4, control constraints allow a biological system to evaluate alternative modes of operation given the state of the system and the environment. Depending on that evaluation they modulate the activity of basic productive constraints in such a way that the system as a whole maintains itself. A regulated biological organization, therefore, does not only establish its own conditions of existence, as described by the notion of closure of constraints. It also operates on how these conditions of existence are realized. The main difference between basic and regulated closure is that the first includes activities that have the effect of maintaining the system, and the second establishes a causal regime that modulates these activities. It selects between its possible actions and takes the selected actions to maintain itself. Including regulation enriches the organizational account of teleology by treating a living organism not only as being teleological but also as operating teleologically (Bich, 2024a).[25]

5.2 Organization and Functions

The account of teleology just discussed provides a philosophical grounding for the organizational account of biological functions. Accounts of biological functions focus on the role of specific traits or parts rather than on the biological system as a whole. According to the organizational framework, in a system that realizes a teleological regime of self-determination, it is possible to ascribe functions to parts. The organizational account of functions was inspired by the work of McLaughlin (2001) and Christensen and Bickhard (2002), among others, and developed in the details by Mossio et al. (2009). The specificity of these contributions is that they relate functions to contributions to the maintenance of the system to which they belong. I will focus in particular on the formulation of this account by Mossio et al. (2009), as it is built on the theoretical framework discussed in the previous sections and complements the account of teleology analyzed in Section 5.1.

The core idea of the organizational account of functions is that in a regime of self-maintenance that realizes closure of constraints and, therefore, is inherently teleological, functional attributions are justified in terms of the contributions of traits to the maintenance of the system that harbors and produces them. More specifically, on this account, a trait or part T exerts a biological function *if and only if* the following conditions are satisfied (Mossio et al., 2009; Saborido et al., 2011):

(1) The organization of the system S to which T belongs realizes closure of constraints (it is a self-maintaining biological organization);
(2) T is produced and maintained under some constraints exerted by the organization of S;
(3) T contributes to the maintenance of the organization of S;
(4) S is organizationally differentiated, that is, there are differential contributions to the maintenance of its organization, which allow for the identification of functions.

---

[25] Recent work by González de Prado and Saborido (2023) follows a different path, ascribing to regulation a non-organizational teleological dimension that is different from the contribution to self-maintenance and possibly complementary to it. It is a version of teleological accounts grounded in biological selection. This work takes a special perspective on regulation, as it focuses on one of the definitory features of regulation (their activity: the first requirement discussed in Section 4) and analyzes regulation detached from the biological organization that harbors it. It argues that regulatory constraints are teleological themselves because they select between different behaviors of basic constraints.

In a system that realizes a self-determining teleological organization, where the telos of the system is understood in terms of self-maintenance, a biological function is therefore understood as a contribution of a part to the maintenance of the organization (e.g. a living cell) that, in turn, contributes to producing and maintaining the part itself (Mossio et al., 2009).[26] An important implication of this account is that given that self-maintenance is characterized in terms of closure of constraints, the functional parts of this type of organization, which contribute to its self-maintenance, coincide with the constraints subject to closure. Hence, for a biological system, the set of constraints subject to closure is the set of biological functions: The basic constraints involved in the causal regime of self-production can be characterized as first-order functions, while regulatory constraints as second or higher-order functions (Bich et al., 2016).

All systems that satisfy these conditions can harbor biological functions. In this view, teleology and function would be linked to any kind of biological system that can be expressed in terms of this type of organization, rather than to the more restrictive concept of organism. In principle this account could attribute functions to supra-organismal systems such as ecosystems (Nunes-Neto et al., 2014) or symbiotic associations (Bich, 2019), if they can be shown to be organizationally closed. It provides a general framework for biological teleology and functions that can in principle account for a wide range of biological systems coming out of interactions between living organisms.

The organizational account of functions is a framework that can be situated in the middle between the two main traditional accounts of biological functions, the dispositional and the etiological ones. It aims to keep their virtues while avoiding the issues usually associated with them. Dispositional accounts (Cummings, 1975) identify the function of a component with its causal role within a larger system. However, they do not provide a normative basis for distinguishing which among many causal effects to count as the function of a component. Like dispositional accounts, the organizational account focuses on the role of components in a system but it characterizes this system in teleological terms, thus grounding principled functional attributions. The etiological approaches based on evolutionary selected effects focus on the origin and explain the presence of functional traits by appealing to their evolutionary history. They identify as functions those effects of components that led the ancestors of current organisms to be selected (Millikan, 1989; Neander, 1991). They face several problems, including that previous adaptations may no longer be functional for the organism, or traits that are currently contributing to the

---

[26] For a proposal on how to address not only functions but also biological malfunctions in organizational terms, see Saborido and Moreno (2015).

survival of an organism might not have been previously selected as adaptations. The organizational framework also aims to explain the presence and origin of a trait, but it does so in terms of its production, maintenance and the role it plays within a biological system. Therefore, it is not subject to the problems confronting evolutionary accounts of function. Moreover, as argued by Frick et al. (2019), it might have some practical advantages. By adopting an etiological evolutionary account, one should expect that when scientists identify a function, they do so on the basis of evolutionary evidence. However, this is not what typically happens in scientific practice. When biologists characterize a function, they may do it on the basis of things happening at the present time within an organism, and only afterwards attempt to reconstruct its evolutionary past.

Within the organizational framework, functional roles are usually attributed to physiological traits involved in the maintenance of the organism. One issue faced by this framework concerns cross-generation functions, that is, those functions, such as reproduction, which do not directly or explicitly contribute to the maintenance of the current organization of a biological system. To address this concern, advocates of the organizational framework have provided a possible yet controversial way to functionally ground cross-generation functions such as reproduction (Saborido et al., 2011, see also Mossio & Pontarotti, 2022). In their view, reproductive traits are functional because they are produced by the biological organization of the parents at some point in their life cycle, and they contribute to reestablishing that very organization in the offspring. The main idea is that if a given system possesses an organization realizing closure because of its causal and material connection with a previous system possessing the same organization, then both systems can be considered as temporal instances of the same encompassing organization. Based on this idea, the solution proposed by Saborido et al. (2011) is that a reproductive function is subject to a regime closure of constraints within a self-maintaining organization whose extension in time goes beyond the lifespan of an individual organism. According to this view, one could say that the sperm cell has the function of inseminating the ovum, because by inseminating the ovum the trait contributes to the replacement of the systems that are part of an organization, which in turn exerts several constraints under which the semen is produced and maintained in time. This account of cross-generation function has raised criticisms, for example, by Artiga and Martinez (2016), who argue that the organizational account is ultimately an etiological account. In a reply to Artiga and Martinez's paper, Mossio and Saborido (2016) agree that the organizational account is compatible with etiological accounts in general, because it also aims to explain the origin and presence of a trait. However, they argue, it constitutes an alternative to those etiological accounts that are based on evolutionary considerations, because it provides a different grounding for functional attributions: maintenance of an organization through generations rather than evolution by natural selection.

6 Interpreting Biological Phenomena through the Lens of Organization

This section addresses attempts to apply the organizational framework to investigate and explain biological phenomena. The common feature of these endeavors is that they address biological phenomena by foregrounding the living systems that realize them. They do so by considering these phenomena within the context of organized cohesive wholes that maintain themselves. This framework has been applied in this way to phenomena such as evolutionary drift (Maturana & Varela, 1987; Maturana & Mpodozis, 2000), multicellularity (Arnellos et al., 2014; Bich et al., 2019; Bechtel & Bich, 2023; Bich, 2024b), intracellular signaling in bacteria (Bich & Bechtel, 2022a), heredity (Mossio & Pontarotti, 2022), development (Montévil et al., 2016; Bich & Skillings, 2023), collective biological organizations (Canciani et al., 2019; Militello et al., 2021), minimal biological agency (Barandiaran et al., 2009; Moreno, 2018), multicellular agency (Arnellos & Moreno, 2015), and ecological systems (Nunes-Neto et al., 2014). For reasons of space not all the biological phenomena addressed by the organizational account can be discussed here. I will focus instead on two cases that exemplify some of the core features of this framework and show how it can be fruitfully applied in biology. The first example is work on origins of life, which perfectly illustrates the focus on the minimal biological organization and the related idea of multiple realizability. The second is biological communication, which represents a direct application of the organizational account of functions to a biological case study.

6.1 Origins of Life

For several decades, origins of life has been the main field of application of the organizational framework in biology, through work based on the notion of autopoiesis (Luisi, 2006). This has been facilitated by two closely interrelated features of this theoretical framework (Bich & Damiano, 2007). The first is the focus on organization as the minimal set of relations common to all living organisms, which makes it a good theoretical tool to investigate minimal life or the steps towards it (Ruiz-Mirazo & Moreno, 2004). The second is the emphasis on organization rather than intrinsic properties of components, which supports the idea of multiple realizability of living systems. To study the origins of life, scientists cannot rely on traces or fossils of prebiotic systems. Nor they can totally rely on knowledge of present-day biological systems to infer the features of precursors of current living systems, because early physical and ecological conditions are not well known. Moreover, at early steps in prebiotic evolution there could have been takeovers by new forms of proto-life, replacing older ones and thus also generating new ecological relationships. This scenario might seem to preclude the possibility of a scientific investigation of the previous steps towards life. However, the idea of multiple realizability allows scientists such as synthetic biologists to attempt to create today possible forms of prebiotic entities without necessarily claiming that they are the true antecedents of contemporary life. Scientists, thus, can investigate the prebiotic world by experimenting with a variety of biologically plausible prebiotic components that are not necessarily the same components of full-fledged living organisms, and to use them to produce models of possible precursors of life. These results, by analogy, can provide useful information about a subset of the general constraints that prebiotic evolution had to satisfy. As such, they do allow scientists to formulate some hypothetical scenarios about the origins of life.

The starting idea of an organizational approach to the origins of life is that biological systems are individuated through their own activities. Advocates of the early organizational framework such as Maturana and Varela (Varela et al., 1974) put emphasis on the presence of a physical border, a membrane generated by the system itself. In the context of research on the origins of life, which was mostly focused on the emergence of replication and reproduction as the conditions for biological evolution, the introduction of the notion of autopoiesis has provided the theoretical basis for a shift in attention towards properties of compartments (Hanczyc, 2009). However, an organizational approach does not just emphasize the importance of experimenting with compartments, but rather the need to integrate metabolism (self-production) and compartmentation (self-distinction from the medium and control over concentrations and exchanges) into a spatially individuated organized system capable of achieving self-maintenance as a whole (Luisi, 1993). This requires a shift from a focus on individual components to one on "protocells" as coherent unities (spherical collections of lipids) with internal processes, proposed as the infrastructures for the origins of life.[27]

Already in the early years of the organizational tradition and of Artificial Life, Francisco Varela introduced the definition of an autopoietic system together with a computational model of the generation and maintenance of a compartment (Varela et al., 1974). One of the first isolated attempts to realize biochemical laboratory experiments based on this theoretical framework was carried out by Gloria Guiloff, a graduate student in Maturana's laboratory at the Universidad de

---

[27] See Rasmussen et al. (2008) for a general picture of work on protocells.

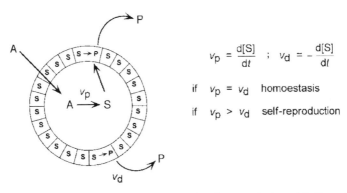

$$v_p = \frac{d[S]}{dt} \quad ; \quad v_d = -\frac{d[S]}{dt}$$

if $\quad v_p = v_d \quad$ homoestasis

if $\quad v_p > v_d \quad$ self-reproduction

Figure 6 The chemical model of the "minimal autopoietic unit" (from Zepik et al., 2001, reproduced with permission from John Wiley & Sons, Inc).

Chile, although without success (Guiloff, 1981). However, it is with the work of Pier Luigi Luisi's group in Zurich first and later in Rome, that these ideas gave rise to a full-fledged research program on origins of life (Stano & Luisi, 2016). Luisi adopted a definition of biological organization based on the work of Maturana and Varela, but minimal enough to be applicable to prebiotic chemical systems: "a system which is spatially defined by a semipermeable compartment of its own making, and which is self-sustaining by transforming external energy/nutrients by its own process of component production" (Luisi, 1998: 619).

Several experiments inspired by this autopoietic definition have been performed by Luisi's group over the decades. A particularly illustrative example is Zepik et al.'s (2001) chemical model of minimal autopoietic unity (Figure 6). This model is designed to explore the relationship between compartments and self-maintenance in prebiotic systems. It describes a compartmentalized chemical system composed of an oleate vesicle, a spherical bilayer structure made of lipids, that hosts an aqueous core. The boundary of the vesicle, the bilayer lipidic structure, is maintained by the continuous replacement of decayed oleic acid components on the surface (P in the figure) by new components (S in the figure) produced through the hydrolysis of a precursor A. The originality of the model does not consist just in the synthesis of the vesicle but in that it combines a reaction of production of membrane components S from A, with a competitive decay reaction which transforms S into the waste product P. By balancing the rates of the two reactions the chemical model can account for different and biologically interesting kinetic modes such as homeostasis (when the rates are equal), growth (when production is faster than decay, eventually leading to division and reproduction), and death (when decay is faster than production).

The minimal chemical model allows for the exploration of different possible dynamic regimes by modulation of these reactions. By focusing on the dynamic organization of simple vesicles, it does not aim to identify what were the actual chemical components of prebiotic systems during the origins of life. It aims instead to provide proof of principle for experimental investigation of possible self-maintaining precursors of current living systems, aimed at achieving a better understanding of the conditions for the emergence of prebiotic organizations.

It is worth mentioning that although these pioneering experiments rely on the idea that living systems share a common self-maintaining organization and aim to discover its minimal requirements, they focus more on fleshing out properties of coherent dynamic wholes than on building organized systems with different parts playing different roles. This is due in great part to technical limitations, and the need to realize reliable compartmentalized systems such as protocells before turning the attention to establishing internal metabolic processes (see Ruiz-Mirazo et al., 2014 for a discussion). The next step consists in designing a basic internal metabolism capable of sustaining itself and synthesizing both the lipids that constitute the membranes of the vesicles and the peptides (short chains of amino acids) to be incorporated into these membranes so as to provide channels through which specific molecules are admitted or expelled from the cell. However, protocell designers recognize also that they must build mechanisms that control the behavior of those channels so as to avoid osmotic crises and to ensure that materials enter and are expelled consistently with the needs of metabolism. More recent work has gone in this direction by providing more sophisticated chemical and computational models of self-maintaining compartments with differentiated components. Examples are models of membranes with simple channels, made of internally produced peptides, that allow the diffusion of metabolites in and out of a vesicle (Ruiz-Mirazo & Mavelli, 2007; Shirt-Ediss et al., 2013). Other work has investigated the possibilities of modeling spatially constrained proto metabolism (Lauber et al., 2023).

6.2 Biological Communication

Let us now move to communication, an example of application of the organizational account of functions to understand a biological phenomenon, carried out by Ramiro Frick and collaborators (Frick et al., 2019). Communication is a very widespread and diversified phenomenon in biology. Bacteria exchange signals and coordinate their activities – for example, through quorum sensing mechanisms like those described in Section 1. When damaged, plants release volatile molecules that are detectable by neighboring plants, which in turn activate preventive defense mechanisms against herbivores. Animals such as mammals or birds can make use of vocalizations. At the edges of biology, communication may include attempts by synthetic biologists to design artificial protocells capable of triggering signaling response in living cells for medical and technological applications (Rampioni et al., 2014).

Quoting Thom Scott-Phillips, "on first appearances, these phenomena have little in common. Yet they must presumably share something, if we are happy to identify them all as instances of communication" (Scott-Phillips, 2009: 245). Theoretical accounts of biological communication aim to identify and unify into a coherent framework the common elements that allow scientists to account for all these phenomena in terms of communication. Besides unification of different phenomena under a common theoretical notion, accounts of communication also need to satisfy two further requirements (Bich & Frick, 2018). The first is an operationability requirement: They should be applicable in science and capable of grounding and orienting theoretical and experimental research on communication in biology as well as in related disciplines such as synthetic biology, where they should also offer guidelines for the evaluation of results. The second is a demarcation requirement: An account of communication should be able to provide conceptual tools to discriminate between communicative and other biological interactions. In fact, not all nonphysical interactions between biological systems that trigger behavioral changes are instances of communication. Let us consider, for example, a lion chasing a gazelle. The lion sees the gazelle and starts chasing it. The gazelle hears the lion approaching and starts running in order to escape it. Then the lion adjusts its course to the new path and speed of the gazelle, and so on. This is a case of interaction in which two biological systems realize a form of coordinated behavior in which actions in one system trigger changes in the behavior of the other, but we would not say that the noise made by the lion is a signal that communicates to the gazelle that it needs to escape. Intuitively, this is not a case of communication.

The two accounts of communication most widely adopted in biology are the "information" and "influence" approaches. According to the information-based approach, communication can be defined in terms of information transfer from a sender to a receiver by means of a signal. Although the characterization of communication in terms of information is widespread, the very concept of "information" is controversial due to the lack of agreement on a common characterization of information, and the demanding theoretical assumptions on notions such as information and representations (Kalkman, 2019). Moreover, this approach puts more emphasis on the informational content of the signal, and less on the role of the system that realizes, harbors, maintains, and employs the mechanisms necessary to engage in communicative interactions. The competing account is based on the notion of influence. According to it, communication can be defined in terms of a signal emitted by a sender: (1) whose presence triggers some response in the receiver; and (2) that has the function of triggering such a response. The influence account emphasizes the operations of the systems involved in communication and does not carry the same heavy theoretical baggage as the information account. Most importantly for organizational theorists it grounds communication in the notion of function. The functional dimension is essential. It provides a criterion to discriminate between cases of communication and other interactions. Going back to the example of the lion-gazelle system, for example, one could not say that the noise made by the lion has the function of triggering the escape of the gazelle. Therefore, according to this view, this is not a case of communication.

The notion of communication as influence was introduced by Dawkins and Krebs (1978) within an evolutionary framework. To ground their account, they adopt an evolutionary-etiological account of biological functions. In their view, the functionality of a signal for the sender is interpreted in terms of adaptations: The ability to send a signal is a functional trait because it allowed the ancestors of the sender to survive and reproduce at a higher rate than other individuals lacking this trait. Formulated in terms of etiological functions, however, this account exhibits several issues. This is due to the fact that it defines an interaction between organisms as communicative only in virtue of a history of selection of similar patterns of interactions realized by their ancestors. In doing so, the influence account risks conflating two different questions: a question about what communication is and how it takes place in a system under study, with a question about how the communicative interaction originated in the first place. As remarked by Di Paolo (1999: 20–21), this approach implies that any interaction between organisms, "no matter how ritualized or similar to known cases of communication," cannot be considered to be an instance of communication until its selective history has been advanced. This is problematic from the point of view of scientific practice inasmuch as many biologists are usually interested in the phenomenon of communication they are currently observing, rather than its evolutionary history. The latter is usually investigated only after the trait in question has already been described as a signal and the interaction that it mediates as an instance of communication. Moreover, this account would exclude from the set of communicative interactions those that are the result of exaptations, even if they exhibit the same phenomenology as those interactions that are the result of selection. Importantly, the characterization of communication as a product of natural selection rules out a priori the very possibility of an artificial, non-evolved communication system, making this approach useless in contexts like synthetic biology where communication is playing an increasingly important role.

A possible solution to these problems, as advocated by Frick et al. (2019), is to reframe the influence approach and the notion of functional influence in terms of the current organization of the system rather than in terms of evolutionary adaptations. This operation can be done by adopting the organizational account of biological functions, according to which, as discussed in Section 5, functions are understood as a contribution of a trait to the maintenance of a biological organization that, in turn, contributes to producing and maintaining the trait itself. By adopting this account, the influence approach to biological communication can be reframed in organizational terms. In this view, to say that a signal is functional means that it contributes to the maintenance of the current organization of the sender, without necessarily appealing to its evolutionary history. Given two systems, A and B, realizing regulated closure of constraints, according to an organizational-influence account communication implies that (1) a receiver B responds to a signal emitted by the sender A, and (2) that a signal is a sender's trait that by triggering some response in a receiver B, contributes to maintain the organization of A that, in turn, is responsible to produce and maintain the signal trait itself.

More specifically, understood in organizational terms, communication relies on the operations of sensory-effector regulatory mechanisms in the two partners, realized by control constraints. Sensors of regulatory mechanisms of the sender A are triggered by internal or environmental conditions, and their effectors activate the emission of a signal by A. The signal triggers a regulatory response in the receiver B, which changes its behavior. The new behavior of B is functional for the sender in the sense that it contributes to the maintenance of A in the context that activated the regulatory action in A. If a pattern of interaction is observed that realizes this type of closed loop, it can be identified as an instance of communication (Figure 7). A simple example is a hungry cub calling for its mother, which responds by bringing food. The cub (the sender A) maintains itself by recruiting a functional contribution from the mother, the receiver B. The same can be said of bacteria interacting through quorum sensing mechanisms while colonizing a surface and forming a biofilm and, in principle, of artificial systems if they satisfy the requirements for functional influence.[28]

The organizational-influence account satisfies the operationability requirement mentioned earlier, as it provides a naturalized notion of communication that can be applied directly to scientific practice. It also satisfies the demarcation requirement inasmuch as it provides tools to discriminate between interactions that are communicative and those that are not. A virtue of this account derives from its focus on current systems, typical of the organizational framework. It makes it possible to identify and to study in the field or in experimental settings as

---

[28] See Frick et al. (2019) and Bich and Frick (2018) for a detailed discussion of case studies from biology and synthetic biology.

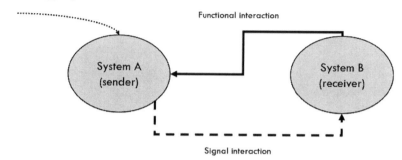

Figure 7 Communication between biological systems A and B. The dotted line represents the conditions triggering regulatory actions in the sender A. The dashed line represents the signal emitted by A on the basis of its regulatory activity. The full line represents a response by B that is functional for A.

instances of communication phenomena that realize interactive patterns typical of signaling interactions despite not being the result of evolutionary adaptations or without the need to reconstruct their evolutionary history.

7 Bridging Philosophical Frameworks: Organization and Mechanisms

This section aims to situate the organizational framework within a wider philosophical context by discussing the relationship with new mechanism, another framework in the philosophy of biology that refers to organization to explain biological phenomena. New mechanism appeals to how components of a mechanism are organized so that their activities produce a phenomenon. This is a different approach than the one pursued by the organizational framework, which instead focuses on how the components of a biological system are organized not within a mechanism but in such a way that they contribute to the maintenance of the living systems that produce them. These two perspectives each identify a form of organization that is employed in living organisms and deploy different decomposition strategies to develop explanations of biological phenomena. This section discusses the differences between these frameworks by arguing that they are not incompatible but complementary. It then shows that biological explanations can benefit from establishing conceptual bridges between the two.[29]

Traditionally, the organizational framework, with its emphasis on considering the living system as a whole and on abstract relations over material components, has been regarded a priori as in opposition to mechanistic accounts and

---

[29] For the detailed discussion of the relationship between organizational framework and new mechanism see Bich and Bechtel (2021, 2022b). See also Gambarotto (2023) for a discussion focused on teleology.

explanations of biological phenomena. The reason is attributed to the fact that mechanistic explanations are reductionistic and focused on the properties of the components. The roots of this attitude lie, in part, in the historical baggage of the opposition between seventeenth-century mechanism and various vitalist, holist, organicist, and systemic approaches that during the subsequent centuries reacted to the application in biology of the Cartesian or LaMettrian conceptions, which regarded animals and humans as machines (see e.g. Letelier et al., 2011; Wolfe, 2014). During the development of the organizational framework, an important role in this regard was played by Rosen's criticism of a specific notion of mechanism, that of Newtonian mechanics. According to Rosen (1985, 1991), Newtonian mechanism tends to separate and isolate different types of causes, and describes systems in terms of sequences of changes of states. As a consequence, it cannot account for causal circularities where components can be both material causes (substrates and products of transformations processes) and efficient causes (carrying out the transformation processes like enzymes do).

What about new mechanism? This framework views biological phenomena as the products of mechanisms that behave as they do because of their constitution (Machamer et al., 2000; Glennan, 2002; Bechtel & Abrahamsen, 2005). At first sight, thus, the focus on "constitution" might support an opposition between the organizational framework and new mechanism. However, new mechanism does not overlook or discard organization. It defines a mechanism relative to a phenomenon as consisting of the parts whose activities and interactions are *organized* in such a way that they are responsible for the phenomenon: It is not just a question of composition. It is true that mechanisms are constituted by distinguishable parts that perform different operations, but such operations need to be connected in order to bring about a phenomenon. Organization is what determines which parts interact with which other parts, in what order, and how they contribute to the behavior of whole mechanisms, and so on (see Glennan, 2017 for examples).

Much of the discussion of organization among new mechanists has focused on ways components can be put together into mechanisms. Much effort has been directed on explaining how components and activities are arranged so as to realize what Machamer et al. (2000) refer to as "productive continuity", whereby the output of each component but the last is taken up by at least one other, thus connecting the parts into a whole. However, accounts of mechanisms differ with respect to the degree of emphasis put on organization. Machamer et al. (2000) emphasize progression from start to termination conditions, but they acknowledge that there can be bifurcations and cycles in between. Glennan (2002: 344) stresses the importance of "direct, invariant, change-relating generalizations" in characterizing the interactions between parts. In Bechtel and Abrahamsen's account of mechanism, organization plays a more decisive role. In their definition of mechanism (2005) organization is more than the connection between the operations of parts, as they emphasize that these activities need to be "orchestrated" within the context of the mechanism. They also draw attention to the fact that biological mechanisms often exhibit nonsequential organization (Bechtel & Abrahamsen, 2009). In advancing their accounts, however, new mechanists have had little to say about whole living systems. Mechanisms are understood as organized parts that together perform the activities required to generate the phenomenon. The focus is on phenomena – with mechanisms construed as each responsible for one phenomenon – not on the role these phenomena and the corresponding mechanisms play in the context of the system that harbors them, benefits from them, and is responsible for their existence. Living systems seem to be treated as simply collections of mechanisms, leaving unexplored the question about how they are integrated into the system.

The organizational framework, on the contrary, does not start with a specific biological phenomenon, but with a biological system characterized as capable of producing its own components and maintaining itself far from equilibrium with its environment. It appeals to the (internal) organization of the system to account for this capacity. Organization here refers to the way production and transformation processes are connected so that they are able to synthesize the components that realize them by using energy and matter from the environment. The organizational framework differs from mechanistic accounts in that it emphasizes the relations that contribute to the existence and maintenance of the system as whole (and of its parts), rather than the generation of a specific phenomenon. Phenomena – such as the example of glucose metabolism and regulation in mammals discussed in Sections 3 and 4 – are analyzed within the context of a system that maintains itself (and consequently maintains the components involved in generating the phenomenon) and characterized in terms of the contribution to the maintenance of the system. A further difference with new mechanism is that by treating the biological system as a whole as the starting point and the main explanatory target, the organizational framework gives priority to identifying what functions are necessary to produce and maintain it and how they depend on one another, not to describing how a specific biological phenomenon is materially realized. These functional relations establish the requirements for the components and allow that any component that meets them will suffice. This does not mean denying the role of materiality, as seen in Section 3, but just that the materiality of the individual components is the distinguishing feature of the system.

Due to the differences in the focus and in the role ascribed to the material properties of components, new mechanists and organizational theorists engage in decomposition in different ways. While organizational theorists have mostly addressed general theoretical questions, the new mechanists have focused on the research strategies employed by scientists to develop explanations: localizing the phenomenon in a mechanism, decomposing it into constituent parts, determining what activities or operations these parts perform, and then determining how the parts are organized to generate the phenomenon. These activities take the mechanism as the relevant unit. Decomposition implies identifying the material components involved in the production of a phenomenon. This, however, is only the first step in developing a mechanistic explanation: Researchers must also recompose it and resituate it in the context in which it operates to establish that the operations of the parts together suffice for producing the phenomenon (Bechtel, 2009). By doing so, research on mechanisms proceeds both top-down from the phenomenon to the constitution of the mechanism and bottom-up to reconstruct the phenomenon for which the mechanism is responsible.

Work on biological organization has not engaged in decomposition in the same way as described by the mechanists. This tradition has privileged approaches that take the whole system as the relevant unit. When they refer to parts of living system, organizational theorists do so functionally in terms of their contribution to the organization of system that they together realize, rather than in terms of material properties. Some advocates of this tradition, such as Rosen (1991), have argued that bottom-up and top-down descriptions may not be just one the inverse of the other, and their results might not coincide. Therefore, starting from the material parts might lead to missing something of the functioning of the whole system. As a consequence, this tradition, especially the early work, has been characterized by a high degree of generality and abstraction from materiality.

Bich and Bechtel (2021, 2022b) have argued that despite the differences and the important insights produced by each separately, the mechanistic and organizational approaches are not mutually exclusive. The common focus on organization makes them complementary, and each can benefit from engagement with the other. While mechanistic approaches can benefit from situating mechanisms in the context of a self-maintaining organization, adopting mechanistic approaches may help to develop organizational theories and explanations by grounding them in an understanding of how different phenomena are actually realized by biological systems.

Three main points of contact favor this mutual engagement. The first point consists of the adoption of a common framework based on constraints. In Section 3, we have seen how constraints figure in the work of organizational theorists as they develop the ideas of closure of constraints and regulatory control. The recent reframing of new mechanism by Winning and Bechtel (2018) is also grounded in the notion of constraint.[30] They consider the components of mechanisms as imposing constraints restricting the flow of free energy. In their view, biological mechanisms are active because they constrain free energy so as to perform work. Therefore, mechanisms should not be understood simply as organized sets of entities and activities. They are characterized as organized sets of constraints that direct the flow of available free energy so as to carry out the work that generates the phenomenon for which the mechanism is taken to be responsible (see also Militello & Moreno, 2018). Constraints constitute a common ground shared by these two frameworks. Reframing mechanisms in terms of constraints provides the conceptual tools to understand them in a system realizing closure of constraints.

The second point is the notion of organizational functions. Mechanists often speak of mechanisms and their parts as performing functions, but the accounts of function traditionally on offer are not sufficiently focused to characterize functions of biological mechanisms (see Section 5.2). Drawing upon the reformulation of mechanisms in terms of constraints, one can adopt the organizational account and characterize the functions of mechanisms in terms of their contributions to the maintenance of specific biological systems. This allows one to explain the existence and operation of a mechanism by referring to its function within the system.[31]

The third point of contact is the focus on control. The reframed account of mechanism developed by Winning and Bechtel (2018) distinguishes between two types of mechanisms: production and control mechanisms. Production mechanisms are those responsible for generating a phenomenon. They perform physiological and behavioral activities such as synthesis of components, generation of movement, and so on. Control mechanisms instead – similarly to control constraints in the organizational framework – are responsible for changing the behavior of other mechanisms. They do so by modifying some of the constraints active in production mechanisms, and they do so on the basis of the measurement of some variables. Most of the mechanisms characterized by the

---

[30] Piekarski (2023) calls it "the constraint-based mechanisms approach."

[31] Other advocates of new mechanism engage in functional analysis in a different way. They do not ascribe functions by referring to the maintenance of the system, but mostly based on a causal role account of functions. In this case, functional analysis is considered as a mechanism "sketch," that helps in the identification of mechanisms (Piccinini & Craver, 2011). It consists of the analysis of a phenomenon or a capacity in terms of the functional properties of a system. It then requires identifying the structures that possess those functional properties and to fit them into mechanisms. However, once functions are associated with the subjacent mechanisms that realize them, the functional description is replaced by the mechanistic one.

new mechanists can be characterized as production mechanisms – they constrain free energy to carry out a productive activity – constructing or degrading something, moving things, and so on. The second type of mechanisms, control mechanisms, also operates as a result of constraining flows of free energy, but they do so to modify constraints in other mechanisms, thereby determining how those mechanisms operate. They direct the activities of production mechanisms. However, in biological systems, control does not just consist in modifying production mechanisms. As seen in Section 4, biological control is performed in such a way as to maintain the organism: It is functional and regulatory. Looking at control mechanisms in context of a self-maintaining system subject to closure is useful to understand why there are control mechanisms in the first place, to flesh out their functional dimension, and understand why production mechanisms need them in order to operate as parts of the system (Bich & Bechtel, 2022a, 2022b). By adopting this perspective, a living system is understood as consisting of the set of mechanisms responsible for generating the phenomena that are needed so that the system is maintained and for doing so when they needed. Control is paramount for this. Control mechanisms perform the measurements of variables that determine whether the activity of a mechanism is needed or not, and then activate or inhibit it accordingly. This important dimension of biological systems would be simply lost if new mechanists treated living systems as simply collections of mechanisms.

Drawing upon these conceptual bridges between the two frameworks, new mechanists can employ insights of the organizational tradition in addressing crucial questions about how to select phenomena, identify components of mechanisms, and generalize mechanistic accounts (Bich & Bechtel, 2021). Let us start with the characterization of phenomena to be explained in terms of mechanisms. A vast number of regularities or repeatable events occur within living systems, yet only some of them are picked out to be explained. What is needed is an account of what to count as a relevant phenomenon and how to identify it. The organizational account of functions may provide criteria from which to select which among the activities occurring in a living system are phenomena to be explained. From an organizational perspective, it would be important to explain those activities that count as functions in virtue of their contribution to the maintenance of the current living system.

Let us then consider the issue of the identification of the components of mechanisms. Once a phenomenon has been selected, one needs criteria to determine which entities constitute the mechanism responsible for the phenomenon, and which do not. Considering as components all those entities that have an effect on the phenomenon would include too many. To establish the boundaries of mechanisms one needs to unbundle a vast network of causally interacting entities to select the relevant ones, with interactions extending also out into the environment. One way to do so is to distinguish control interactions from those taking place within controlled mechanisms. This can be done by focusing on what a mechanism is doing. Considering whether a mechanism operates on other mechanisms (control) provides a principled way of drawing the boundaries of production and control mechanisms. In the specific case of control mechanisms, a further way to establish boundaries is to consider that they perform measurements. Entities whose features are being measured have an effect on the mechanism, but they are not parts of it.

Moving to generalizations, a further challenge confronting new mechanists derives from the fact that research on mechanisms is usually focused on specific instances of a mechanism, often realized in a specific system. Mechanistic explanations, however, rely on regularities and aim to extrapolate from specific cases, and abstract from details, to provide generalizations. One way to do so is to identify phylogenetic relations between instances of a mechanism in different systems. However, differences between mechanisms (or between the organisms harboring them) that have emerged during a history of adaptations might make it unclear whether or not it is possible to extrapolate and generalize. The organizational framework offers a possible solution by considering whether different instances of a mechanism in different systems serve the maintenance of the organism in the same way. If they do not, the differences may not allow generalizations. If the instances of the mechanism contribute to the maintenance of the organism in the same manner, the extrapolation from one system to the other is justified. The same holds for abstractions. If abstracting from the specific details of a mechanism still allows researchers to explain how it performs its function in the system, then the result can be in principle used to develop generalizations.

From the point of view of the organizational framework, one of the main advantages of engaging with new mechanism consists in the possibility to overcome the high degree of abstraction and develop better biological explanations grounded in materiality. Organizational theorists can ground their accounts in an understanding of the mechanisms employed in achieving and maintaining closure. This does not imply abandoning the top-down strategy that starts with the identification of functions and then of the components that realize them. Components can still be characterized primarily in terms of how they contribute to the maintenance of the system, instead of their structural features. However, engaging with new mechanism provides further tools to proceed down to material processes and constraints to explain how they are produced and maintained and what role they play within the system.

Employing the revised notion of mechanism as organized sets of constraints may also contribute to providing better and more precise biological explanations and functional attributions. According to the organizational framework, the entities responsible for those biological activities that would coincide with biological functions are individual constraints (Mossio et al., 2009). More precisely, each functional activity is performed by a constraint, and closure consists in the mutual dependence between these functional constraints. As argued by Bich and Bechtel (2021), identifying a constraint with a biological function may be an abstraction. While useful in some cases for explanatory purposes, nonetheless it risks overlooking the complexity underlying the realization of biological functions and how this complexity matters for the overall functioning of the system. This can be seen already in the relatively simple case of an enzyme, which is often used as a paradigmatic example of functional constraint. The different parts of the enzyme, such as the catalytic site, the phosphorylation and allosteric sites, structures that undergo conformational changes, and so on, contribute differently to the function performed by the enzyme. This function might be better characterized in terms of a mechanism employing several interacting constraints rather than one monolithic constraint. This is even more relevant in multicellular organisms, where the activity of organs depends on the interaction of different structures or cell types constituting them. Let us think of the muscles, valves, and so on, that constitute the heart, or alpha and beta cells, among others, in the pancreas. Signaling control pathways are another example. They are present in all living systems and play different functional roles as a result of being differently regulated in different parts of the system on the basis of the state of the system or the environment. Pathways are usually characterized by several steps in which the various parts involved sense variations and act in turn on other parts accordingly. They often branch and affect distinct parts or establish crosstalk with other pathways. Let us think, for example, of all the steps involved in the release of insulin and the control of glucose metabolism in glycemia regulation: from sensing the energetic state of the system by pancreatic beta cells and the activation of the molecular machinery for the release of insulin into the blood, to the action of insulin in the metabolism of the receiving cells. Each step in this pathway can be also subject to control exerted by constraints from other pathways. This phenomenon might be better understood in terms of sets of constraints organized into mechanisms, rather than as one constraint (insulin or beta cells) acting upon glucose metabolism.

8 Open Challenges: Symbiotic Associations and the Environment

In the previous sections, we have seen how several objections have been advanced to different aspects of the organizational framework, both from without and within the community working on it. Some put into question the possibility of univocally operationalizing constraints (Cusimano & Steiner, 2020) and the capability to ground cross-generation functions (Artiga & Martinez, 2016). Others criticize functional attributions in terms of self-maintenance as too liberal (Garson, 2017), or the very notion of closure as too abstract to provide detailed biological explanations and account for the complexity of biological systems (Bich & Bechtel, 2021, 2022b), and so on. Some of these criticisms have been addressed by organizational theorists, others not yet. In this section, I will conclude by discussing two challenges to the application of an organizational framework in biology, which derive from its distinctive inward-looking perspective focused on the internal organization of biological systems and on the notion of self-maintenance: symbiotic associations and the characterization of the environment. Both have to do with how to understand living systems in a wider context. These challenges have not been extensively addressed by organizational theorists, but I will sketch some possible ways to face them based on existing literature.

8.1 Symbiosis

The first challenge is presented by the debate on biological individuality in the light of new studies on highly integrated collective or composite entities arising out of interactions, from biofilms to holobionts (multicellular hosts with all their associated microbes), from colonies to social insects. Historically, the organizational framework has been developed and applied in biology usually by having in mind organisms as the main target, and by relying on the identification of physical boundaries (such as membranes) and on the use of notions such as closure in order to identify and characterize living systems. However, recent research on complex and highly heterogeneous biological associations such as host-microbiota and, more generally, symbiotic relationships characterized by close functional ties, seems to put into questions the possibility of establishing clear (functional) boundaries for biological systems (Bosch & McFall-Nagai, 2011; Gilbert et al., 2012; Skillings, 2016). Or at least it calls for further work on characterization of the different ways functional interactions can be established within a system or between systems.

Although at first sight these cases might be seen as problematic for the organizational framework, it is not necessarily the case. It is important first to clarify that organizational closure does not imply independence or self-sufficiency. In principle, closure is not incompatible with forms of dependence, and a system can be self-maintaining in the sense that it realizes closure even though it is not independent from other systems or its environment. However, very tight dependencies such as those implied by some symbiotic associations may require specific discussion. Although more work is needed, a possible response to this challenge can be found in the very characterization of an integrated system provided by the organizational framework. In this view, subsystems contribute to one another's conditions of existence by mutually controlling their functional processes in such a way as to achieve closure (Bich, 2024b). This very general idea allows one not only to understand living systems such as organisms as cohesive entities (i.e. individuals), but also to account for those interactions between different biological systems that are necessary for the maintenance of the systems involved, without the need to put into question core notions such as closure (Bich, 2019). Let us see it in more detail.

Regulated closure of constraints is characterized as a causal regime of mutually dependent constraints that determines and modulates a subset of its own conditions of existence, not all of them. One implication is that identifying a system satisfying these conditions does not require identifying all the possible interactions, but just a set of mutually dependent constraints that realize a form of self-maintenance: a minimal loop between constraints. Another implication is that once mutual dependence between constraints is realized within a system, thus achieving closure, this self-maintaining system can have functional interactions with other biological systems. As argued in Bich (2019), among those interactions some can take the form of a mutual dependence between (basic or control) constraints built by the two systems. Given two biological systems A and B realizing closure, system A constrains processes in system B while B also constrains processes in A. By doing so, they are achieving some form of integration across systems, and possibly realizing a new super-organismal organization.[32] If this new organization satisfies the requirements for closure of constraints, it constitutes a new (higher-level) regime of closure (Montévil & Mossio, 2015).

It is worth emphasizing that doing so does not imply per se that once they establish these interactions, the organisms involved are not able to realize organizational closure by themselves anymore. It means, instead, that while maintaining closure as functionally cohesive entities, biological systems can extend their functional networks of constraints by realizing nested integrated causal regimes that include more than one system.[33]

---

[32] This scenario is different from the phenomenon of biological communication discussed in Section 6. The organizational account of communication as influence does not imply the degree of integration required by higher levels of closure, according to which systems or subsystems directly control one another's physiological processes by exchanging constraints. Each partner in a communicative interaction controls its own physiological processes. What happens in the case of communication is that a signal emitted by one of the partners is sensed by the other and triggers a behavioral reaction in the receiver which is functional for the sender. The two communicating partners are not building a larger system subject to closure.

[33] Montévil and Mossio (2015) use the expression "higher level closure" for cases of nested closure such as cells in a multicellular system and use the expression "tendency to closure" to refer to the degree of functional dependence between systems.

How this is done and what are its implications needs to be evaluated case by case depending on the types of interactions between the systems involved (see e.g. Bich, 2019 and Skillings, 2019). Let us consider two examples to illustrate different scenarios in which such an evaluation could be carried out. Eukaryotic organelles of endosymbiotic origin such as mitochondria and chloroplasts, for example, might be considered as cases resulting from an evolutionary process in which one of the partners lost the capability to realize closure of constraints while the other, the host cells, kept it and incorporated the symbionts as organelles into its own regime of closure. In this case, interactions between two systems gave rise to one system realizing closure. Current cases of intracellular endosymbiosis are instead possible candidates to be evaluated as systems realizing higher-level closure of constraints if a mutual dependence in terms of constraints can be identified, as each partner engages in functional interactions without stopping to realize an internal regime of closure.

8.2 Biological Organization and the Environment

Let us move now to the second challenge: the characterization of the environment. One possible worry about the organizational framework is that it may be too focused on the living system, and only considers the environment through the notion of thermodynamic openness, as a necessary yet generic source of matter and energy, or as a source of noise and perturbations to be counteracted. However, the organizational framework can deploy two possible strategies to consider and better characterize the environment: an adaptivity strategy and an ecosystems strategy.

The first strategy, pursued by Menatti and collaborators (Menatti et al., 2022), is inspired by the notion of adaptivity introduced by Di Paolo (2005) and developed in the organizational account of regulatory control (Bich et al., 2016). Adaptivity is defined by Di Paolo as the capability of a system, such as an organism, to remain viable in its environment by regulating itself. It designates the ability of a system to cope with changes in the environment. As discussed in Section 4, this idea has been developed into an account of regulatory control of the activity of those constraints responsible for generating the internal dynamics and behavior of a system, by modulating them in relation to variations in internal and external conditions. Such modulation is carried out by means of specialized constraints or mechanisms that evaluate perturbations and operate accordingly.

To provide a characterization of the environment, Menatti et al. (2022) focus on the fact that regulatory adaptivity enables the organism to actively engage with the environment by promoting change.[34] According to this approach, the

---

[34] The main target of this work is the relationship between environment and health.

environment is characterized relationally, in terms of the type of evaluation operated by living systems under variable conditions and the actions they take. A biological system needs to manage interactions with the environment in such a way as to maintain itself viable. It does so through regulatory control by making decisions based on what it senses in its surroundings. From this perspective, the environment of a system ceases to be a set of independent boundary conditions or a generic source of noise. It is seen as a source of different types of opportunities that allow a system to modify itself to maintain or expand its range of viability. This can be achieved by modifying the system itself, or by acting in and modulating the surroundings to promote their conditions of existence so as to create more supportive ones.

In this view, an environment can be categorized by a system according to how interactions unfold and what types of changes a system can carry out during them. Some interactions with the environment might require specific operations aimed at counteracting or compensating for the effects of the interaction. Most of them would require the system to change its current regime in specific ways to take advantage of them. Let us think, for example, of the light and dark cycle, and the importance it holds in different ways by enabling different activities for photosynthetic organisms or nocturnal animals. For some other systems this very cycle might not be relevant, as it would not trigger regulatory activities. By accounting for these differences, this approach aims to provide a fine-grained characterization of the environment of a living system or group of systems by focusing on the interface between a system's regulatory capabilities and the properties and dynamics taking place in its surroundings.

The second strategy – the ecosystems strategy pursued by El-Hani and collaborators (Nunes-Neto et al., 2014; El-Hani & Nunes-Neto, 2020; El-Hani et al., submitted) – also employs the conceptual tools of the organizational frameworks. But it zooms out from the relationship between the inner operations of living systems and properties of the surroundings to focus on larger networks of interacting entities that include living systems and abiotic elements, collectively operating on fluxes of matter and energy. It looks at interactions *within* the environment of living systems: at how an ecosystem is organized and can be identified, and at how to evaluate if entities can be included in it or not.

The basis for doing this is constituted by the organizational account of ecological functions (Nunes-Neto et al., 2014). This account proposes the thesis that ecological interactions between organisms can realize a form of collective closure between organisms, whose self-maintaining regime goes beyond the individual organisms. This interspecies collective regime of organizational closure is realized by means of mutual constraints exerted by groups of organisms on one another's *external* boundary conditions. It is different from the regime of closure realized within living organisms because in principle it does not involve regulatory control modulating the operation of its parts. It involves only basic constraints exerted by different ecological communities on the environmental flux of matter and energy crossing the larger system. On this account, if an ecological system can be shown to realize a regime of closure, then this regime can be used to ground functional attributions in terms of contribution of the participants to the more comprehensive ecological organization (Nunes-Neto et al., 2014).

The example employed to illustrate this possibility is the interaction between bromeliad plants and their associated organisms such as spiders that live and hunt on it, larvae and adults of mosquitos, and microorganisms (Figure 8). The plant exerts constraints on the external conditions of the animals. It provides spiders with the structural support for building their webs, and it realizes structures that allow the accumulation of water (phytotelmata) where larvae of mosquitos and microorganisms can thrive. The spiders in turn constrain the conditions of existence of the plant: They canalize the flux of nitrogen by hunting mosquitos. Nitrogen, proteins, and amino acids contained in the spiders' carcasses and feces, as well as in the preys' carcasses that fall into the phylotemata, are processed by microorganisms and absorbed by the plant and by the mosquitos, which in turn are eaten by the spiders. If these relations can be characterized in terms of closure, then according to this account each of these entities can be said to be exerting a function.[35]

This account provides a perspective from which to look at the organization of the environment. By doing so, it allows organizational theorists to make fine-grained distinctions in an otherwise generic medium. It also grounds distinctions between environmental constraints that are part of a given ecological organization or external to it. In this view, to be included in the system, an entity should be a constraint that is both dependent on other constraints in the system and enabling the activity of other constraints in it (El-Hani et al., submitted). Such constraints can be directly exerted by living organisms but also by abiotic entities (El-Hani & Nunes-Neto, 2020). In this view an abiotic

---

[35] Lean (2021) criticizes this approach by arguing that it might be impossible to identify cases of closure in ecological systems, apart from very special cases such as this, usually restricted to the interaction of two or few more species in a very narrow and spatially contiguous niche. El-Hani et al. (2023) respond to this criticism by arguing that difficulties stem from the fact that organizationally closed systems show different degrees of cohesion, and ecological systems are situated among the less integrated ones. Therefore, one cannot expect the same degree of cohesiveness found within living organisms. In order to identify an ecological system as organizational closed, it is sufficient to include just part of the constraints exerting influence over the system, but sufficient to give rise to a causal loop. It does not require to extend the scope of the analysis to include all possible constraints involved.

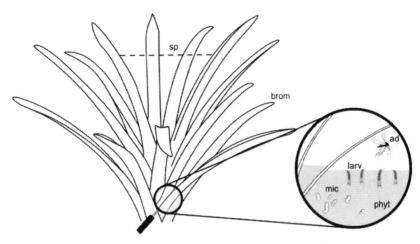

Figure 8 A bromeliad plant and its associated organisms (from Nunes-Neto et al., 2014, reproduced with permission from Springer Nature).

item such as fire interacting with vegetation can be a functional component of an ecosystem's organization if it is subject to closure within that system, that is, if it is both a dependent (i.e. subject to constraints internal to the system) and enabling constraint (i.e. affecting its dynamic and contributing to the maintenance of the system). An item (biotic or abiotic) is external to the system, instead, if it is only a boundary condition not directly dependent on the system.

The adaptivity and ecosystems approaches to the environment are linked because both depend on a living system's capabilities to exert control on its external conditions of existence. One builds upon the internal regulated closure of constraint of living systems and how it allows establishing different types of interactions with the surroundings, thus letting its different features emerge from a background noise. The other identifies a basic regime of closure realized between living systems. The distinctive feature of the ecological strategy is its focus on what systems do that constrains the external conditions of existence of other living systems, either by directly harnessing the external flux of matter and energy, or indirectly by generating external constrains in the environment (e.g. bird nests, spider webs, beaver dams, etc.).

In this final section, I discussed just two of the possible challenges faced by the organizational framework. More challenges and criticisms are going to appear that need to be addressed. After all, this is still a recent approach in the philosophy of biology, pursued by a relatively small, although growing, community of researchers. The development of the organizational framework is an ongoing endeavor, undergoing reframing such as the formulation of closure in terms of constraints and the incorporation of regulatory control. This process is accompanied by the revision of core notions such as function and teleology or closure itself. There is still more work to do to improve an understanding of living systems from an organizational perspective, to provide explanations of biological phenomena, and to further develop and revise the framework to better account for the complexity of living systems.

References

Alon, U. (2007). Network motifs: Theory and experimental approaches. *Nature Review Genetics*, 8(6), 450–461.

Arnellos, A., & Moreno, A. (2015). Multicellular agency: An organizational view. *Biology & Philosophy*, 30(3), 333–357.

Arnellos, A., Moreno, A., & Ruiz-Mirazo, K. (2014). Organizational requirements for multicellular autonomy: Insights from a comparative case study. *Biology & Philosophy*, 29(6), 851–884.

Artiga, M., & Martinez, M. (2016). The organizational account of function is an etiological account of function. *Acta Biotheoretica*, 64(2), 105–117.

Ashby, W. R. (1956). *An Introduction to Cybernetics*. London: Chapman & Hall.

Barandiaran, X., Di Paolo, E., & Rohde, M. (2009). Defining agency: Individuality, normativity, asymmetry and spatio-temporality in action. *Adaptive Behavior*, 17(5), 367–386.

Bechtel, W. (2008). *Mental Mechanisms: Philosophical Perspectives on Cognitive Neurosciences*. New York: Routledge.

Bechtel, W. (2009). Looking down, around, and up: Mechanistic explanation in psychology. *Philosophical Psychology*, 22(5), 543–564.

Bechtel, W., & Abrahamsen, A. (2005). Explanation: A mechanist alternative. *Studies in History and Philosophy of Biological and Biomedical Sciences*, 36(2), 421–441.

Bechtel, W., & Abrahamsen, A. (2009). Complex biological mechanisms: Cyclic, oscillatory, and autonomous. In C. A. Hooker, ed., *Philosophy of Complex Systems: Handbook of the Philosophy of Science*. New York: Elsevier, pp. 257–285.

Bechtel, W., & Bich, L. (2021). Grounding cognition: Heterarchical control mechanisms in biology. *Philosophical Transactions of the Royal Society B: Biological Sciences*, 376(1820), 20190751.

Bechtel, W., & Bich, L. (2023). Using neurons to maintain autonomy: Learning from *C. elegans*. *BioSystems*, 232, 105017.

Bich, L. (2019). The problem of functional boundaries in prebiotic and inter-biological systems. In G. Minati, E. Pessa, & M. Abram, eds., *Systemics of Incompleteness and Quasi-Systems*. New York: Springer, pp. 295–302.

Bich, L. (2024a). Organisational teleology 2.0: Grounding biological purposiveness in regulatory control. *Ratio*. https://doi.org/10.1111/rati.12405.

Bich, L. (2024b). Integrating multicellular systems: Physiological control and degrees of biological individuality. *Acta Biotheoretica*, 72, 1.

Bich, L., & Bechtel, W. (2021). Mechanism, autonomy and biological explanation. *Biology & Philosophy*, 36(6), 53.

Bich, L., & Bechtel, W. (2022a). Control mechanisms: Explaining the integration and versatility of biological organisms. *Adaptive Behavior*, 30(5), 389–407.

Bich, L., & Bechtel, W. (2022b). Organization needs organization: Understanding integrated control in living organisms. *Studies in History and Philosophy of Science*, 93, 96–106.

Bich, L., & Damiano, L. (2007). Theoretical and artificial construction of the living: Redefining the approach from an autopoietic point of view. *Origins of Life Evolution of the Biospheres*, 37, 459–464.

Bich, L., & Damiano, L. (2008). Order in the nothing: Autopoiesis and the organizational characterization of the living. In I. Licata, & A. Sakaji, eds., *Physics of Emergence and Organization*. Singapore: World Scientific, pp. 343–373.

Bich, L., & Frick, R. (2018). Synthetic modelling of biological communication: A theoretical and operational framework for the investigation of minimal life and cognition. *Complex Systems*, 27(3), 267–287.

Bich, L., Mossio, M., Ruiz-Mirazo, K., & Moreno, A. (2016). Biological regulation: Controlling the system from within. *Biology & Philosophy*, 31(2), 237–265.

Bich, L., Mossio, M., & Soto, A. (2020). Glycemia regulation: From feedback loops to organizational closure. *Frontiers in Physiology*, 11, 69.

Bich, L., Pradeu, T., & Moreau, J. F. (2019). Understanding multicellularity: The functional organization of the intercellular space. *Frontiers in Physiology*, 10, 1170.

Bich, L., & Skillings, D. (2023). There are no intermediate stages: An organizational view of development. In M. Mossio, ed., *Organization in Biology*. New York: Springer, pp. 241–262.

Bitbol, M., & Luisi, P. L. (2004). Autopoiesis with or without cognition: Defining life at its edge. *Journal of the Royal Society Interface*, 1, 99–107.

Bosch, T. C. G., & McFall-Nagai, M. J. (2011). Metaorganisms as the new frontier. *Zoology*, 144(4), 185–190.

Canciani, M., Arnellos, A., & Moreno, A. (2019). Revising the superorganism: An organizational approach to complex eusociality. *Frontiers in Psychology*, 10, 2653.

Cannon, W. B. (1929). Organization for physiological homeostasis. *Physiological Reviews*, 9, 399–431.

Christensen, W., & Bickhard, M. (2002). The process dynamics of normative function. *The Monist*, 85(1), 3–28.

Cohen, S. E., & Golden, S. S. (2015). Circadian rhythms in cyanobacteria. *Microbiology and Molecular Biology Review*, 79, 373–385.

Cornish-Bowden, A. (2006). Putting the systems back into systems biology. *Perspectives in Biology and Medicine*, 49(4), 475–489.

Cornish-Bowden, A., & Cárdenas, M. L. (2020). Contrasting theories of life: Historical context, current theories: In search of an ideal theory. *Biosystems*, 188, 104063.

Cummins, R. (1975). Functional analysis. *Journal of Philosophy*, 72, 741–765.

Cusimano, S., & Sterner, B. (2020). The objectivity of organizational functions. *Acta Biotheoretica*, 68(2), 253–269.

Dawkins, R., & Krebs, J. R. (1978). Animal signals: Information or manipulation? In R. Krebs, & N. B. Davies, eds., *Behavioural Ecology: An Evolutionary Approach*. Sutherland: Sinauer Associates, pp. 282–309.

Di Frisco, J., & Mossio, M. (2020). Diachronic identity in complex life cycles: An organisational perspective. In A. S. Meincke, & J. Dupré, eds., *Biological Identity: Perspectives from Metaphysics and the Philosophy of Biology*. New York: Routledge, pp. 177–199.

Di Paolo, E. (1999). *On the evolutionary and behavioral dynamics of social coordination: Models and theoretical aspects*. Doctoral dissertation, University of Sussex.

Di Paolo, E. (2005). Autopoiesis, adaptivity, teleology, agency. *Phenomenology and the Cognitive Sciences*, 4(4), 429–452.

Dresow, M., & Love, A. C. (2023). Teleonomy: Revisiting a proposed conceptual replacement for teleology. *Biological Theory*, 18(2), 101–113.

El-Hani, C. N., Coutinho, J. G. E., & Leite, C. M. P. (2025). Closure of constraints and the individuation of causal systems in biology. In P. Illaris, & F. Russo, eds., *Routledge Handbook of Philosophy of Causality and Causal Methods*. New York: Routledge (In press).

El-Hani, C. N., & Nunes-Neto, N. F. (2020). Life on Earth is not a passenger, but a driver: Explaining the transition from a physicochemical to a life-constrained world from an organizational perspective. In L. Baravalle, & L. Zaterka, eds., *Life and Evolution – Latin American Essays on the History and Philosophy of Biology*. New York: Springer, pp. 69–84.

El-Hani, C. N., Rebelo Gomes de Lima, F., & Nunes-Neto, N. (2023). From the organizational theory of ecological functions to a new notion of sustainability. In M. Mossio, ed., *Organization in Biology*. New York: Springer, pp. 285–328.

Etxeberria, A., & Umerez, J. (2006). Organismo y organización en la Biología Teórica ¿Vuelta al organicismo? Organism and organization in theoretical biology: Back to organicism? *Ludus Vitalis*, 14(26), 3–38.

Fell, D. A. (1997). *Understanding the Control of Metabolism*. Portland: Portland University Press.

Frick, R., Bich, L., & Moreno, A. (2019). An organisational approach to biological communication. *Acta Biotheoretica*, 67(2), 103–128.

Gambarotto, A. (2023). Teleology and mechanism: A dialectical approach. *Synthese*, 201(5), 155.

Gambarotto, A., & Mossio, M. (2024). Enactivism and the Hegelian stance on intrinsic purposiveness. *Phenomenology and the Cognitive Sciences*, 23, 155–177.

Gambarotto, A., & Nahas, A. (2022). Teleology and the organism: Kant's controversial legacy for contemporary biology. *Studies in History and Philosophy of Science*, 93, 47–56.

Ganti, T. (1975). Organization of chemical reactions into dividing and metabolizing units: The chemotons. *Biosystems*, 7, 15–21.

Garson, J. (2017). Against organizational functions. *Philosophy of Science*, 84, 1093–1103.

Gilbert, S., & Sarkar, S. (2000). Embracing complexity: Organicism for the 21st century. *Developmental Dynamics*, 9, 1–9.

Gilbert, S. F., Sapp, J., & Tauber, A. I. (2012). A symbiotic view of life: We have never been individuals. *The Quarterly Review of Biology*, 87(4), 325–341.

Glansdorf, P., & Prigogine, I. (1971). *Thermodynamic Theory of Structure, Stability and Fluctuations*. London: Wiley.

Glennan, S. (2002). Rethinking mechanistic explanations. *Philosophy of Science*, 69(3), 342–353.

Glennan, S. (2017). *The New Mechanical Philosophy*. Oxford: Oxford University Press.

González de Prado, J., & Saborido, C. (2023). Biological purposes beyond natural selection: Self-regulation as a source of teleology. *Erkenntnis*. https://doi.org/10.1007/s10670-023-00695-2.

Green, S., & Jones, N. (2016). Constraint-based reasoning for search and explanation: Strategies for understanding variation and patterns in biology. *Dialectica*, 70(3), 343–374.

Green, S., & Wolkenhauer, O. (2013). Tracing organizing principles: Learning from the history of systems biology. *History and Philosophy of the Life Sciences*, 35(4), 553–576.

Guiloff, G. D. (1981). Autopoiesis and neobiogenesis. In M. Zeleny, ed., *Autopoiesis: A Theory of Living Organization*. New York: North Holland, pp. 118–125.

Hagen, J. (2021). *Life out of Balance: Homeostasis and Adaptation in a Darwinian World*. Tuscaloosa: The University of Alabama Press.

Hanczyc, M. (2009). The early history of protocells: The search for the recipe of life. In S. Rasmussen, M. Bedau, L. Chen et al., eds., *Protocells Bridging Nonliving and Living Matter*. Cambridge, MA: MIT Press, pp. 3–17.

Jacob, F. (1970). *La logique du vivant: Une historie de l'hérédité*. Paris: Gallimard.

Jonas, H. (1953). A critique of cybernetics. *Social Research*, 20, 172–192.

Kalkman, D. (2019). New problems for defining animal communication in informational terms. *Synthese*, 196(8), 3319–3336.

Kant, I. (1790/1987). *Critique of Judgment*. Indianapolis: Hackett.

Kauffman, S. (2000). *Investigations*. Oxford: Oxford University Press.

Klir, G. (1991). *Facets of Systems Science*. New York: Kluwer.

Larson, B., Ruiz-Herrero, T., Lee, S., et al. (2020). Biophysical principles of choanoflagellate self-organization. *Proceedings of the National Academy of Sciences*, 117(3), 1303–1311.

Lauber, N., Tichacek, O., Narayanankutty, K., De Martino, D., & Ruiz-Mirazo, K. (2023). Collective catalysis under spatial constraints: Phase separation and size-scaling effects on mass action kinetics. *Physical Review E*, 108(4), 044410.

Lean, C. H. (2021). Invasive species and natural function in ecology. *Synthese*, 198, 9315–9333.

Letelier, J. C., Cardenas, M. L., & Cornish-Bowden, A. (2011). From L'Homme machine to metabolic closure: Steps towards understanding life. *Journal of Theoretical Biology*, 286, 100–113.

Levy, A., & Bechtel, W. (2013). Abstraction and the organization of mechanisms. *Philosophy of Science*, 80(2), 241–261.

Luisi, P. L. (1993). Defining the transition to life: Self-replicating bounded structures and chemical autopoiesis. In W. Stein, & F. J. Varela, eds., *Thinking about Biology: An Invitation to Current Theoretical Biology*. Reading: Addison Wesley, pp. 17–40.

Luisi, P. L. (1998). About various definitions of life. *Origins of Life and Evolution of the Biosphere*, 28, 613–622.

Luisi, P. L. (2006). *The Emergence of Life: From Chemical Origins to Synthetic Biology*. Cambridge: Cambridge University Press.

Machamer, P., Darden, L., & Craver, C. F. (2000). Thinking about mechanisms. *Philosophy of Science*, 67, 1–25.

Maturana, H. (1978). Biology of language. In G. A. Miller, & E. Lenneberg, eds., *Psychology and Biology of Language and Thought: Essays in Honour of Eric Lenneberg*. New York: Academic Press, pp. 27–63.

Maturana, H. (1980). Biology of cognition. In H. Maturana, & F. J. Varela, eds., *Autopoiesis and Cognition: The Realization of the Living*. Dordrecht: Reidel, pp. 1–58.

Maturana, H., & Mpodozis, J. (2000). The origin of species by means of natural drift. *Revista Chilena de Historia Natural*, 73(2), 261–310.

Maturana, H., & Varela, F. J. (1980). Autopoiesis: The organization of the living. In H. Maturana, & F. J. Varela, eds., *Autopoiesis and Cognition: The Realization of the Living*. Dordrecht: Reidel, pp. 59–145.

Maturana, H., & Varela, F. J. (1987). *The Tree of Knowledge*. Boston: Shambhala

McCulloch, W. (1974). Recollections of the many sources of cybernetics. *ASC Forum*, VI(2), 5–16.

McLaughlin, P. (2001). *What Functions Explain: Functional Explanation and Self-Reproducing Systems*. Cambridge: Cambridge University Press.

Menatti, L., Bich, L., & Saborido, C. (2022). Health and environment from adaptation to adaptivity: A situated relational account. *History and Philosophy of the Life Sciences*, 44(3), 38.

Militello, G., Bich, L., & Moreno, A. (2021). Functional integration and individuality in prokaryotic collective organisations. *Acta Biotheoretica*, 69(3), 391–415.

Militello, G., & Moreno, A. (2018). Structural and organisational conditions for being a machine. *Biology and Philosophy*, 33, 35.

Millikan, R. G. (1989). In defense of proper functions. *Philosophy of Science*, 56, 288–302.

Monod, J. (1970). *Les hasard et la necessité*. Paris: Seuil.

Monod, J., Chengeux, J. P., Jacob, F. (1963). Allosteric proteins and cellular control systems. *Journal of Molecular Biology*, 6, 306–329.

Montévil, M., & Mossio, M. (2015). Biological organisation as closure of constraints. *Journal of Theoretical Biology*, 372, 179–191.

Montévil, M., Mossio, M., Pocheville, A., & Longo, G. (2016). Theoretical principles for biology: Variation. *Progress in Biophysics and Molecular Biology*, 122, 36–50.

Montévil, M., Speroni, L., Sonnenschein, C., & Soto, A. M. (2016). Modeling mammary organogenesis from biological first principles: Cells and their physical constraints. *Progress in Biophysics and Molecular Biology*, 122, 58–69.

Moreno, A. (2018). On minimal autonomous agency: Natural and artificial. *Complex Systems*, 27(3), 289–313.

Moreno, A., & Mossio, M. (2015). *Biological Autonomy: A Philosophical and Theoretical Enquiry*. New York: Springer.

Mossio, M. (2023). Introduction: Organization as a scientific blind spot. In M. Mossio, ed., *Organization in Biology*. New York: Springer, pp. 1–22.

Mossio, M., & Bich, L. (2017). What makes biological organisation teleological? *Synthese*, 194(4), 1089–1114.

Mossio, M., Bich, L., & Moreno, A. (2013). Emergence, closure and inter-level causation in biological systems. *Erkenntnis*, 78(2), 153–178.

Mossio, M., Montévil, M., & Longo, G. (2016). Theoretical principles for biology: Organization. *Progress in Biophysics and Molecular Biology*, 122(1), 24–35.

Mossio, M., & Pontarotti, G. (2022). Conserving functions across generations: Heredity in light of biological organization. *The British Journal for the Philosophy of Science*, 73(1), 249–278.

Mossio, M., & Saborido, C. (2016). Functions, organization and etiology: A reply to Artiga and Martinez. *Acta Biotheoretica*, 64(3), 263–275.

Mossio, M., Saborido, C., & Moreno, A. (2009). An organizational account of biological functions. *The British Journal for the Philosophy of Science*, 60(4), 813–841.

Nahas, A., & Sachs, C. (2023). What's at stake in the debate over naturalizing teleology? An overlooked metatheoretical debate. *Synthese*, 201(4), 142.

Neander, K. (1991). Functions as selected effects: The conceptual analyst's defence. *Philosophy of Science*, 58, 168–184.

Nicholson, D. (2014). The return of the organism as a fundamental explanatory concept in biology. *Philosophy Compass*, 9(5), 347–359.

Nunes-Neto, N., Moreno, A., & El Hani, C. N. (2014). Function in ecology: An organizational approach. *Biology & Philosophy*, 29(1), 123–141.

Pattee, H. (1972). The nature of hierarchical controls in living matter. In R. Rosen, ed., *Foundations of Mathematical Biology Volume I Subcellular Systems*. New York: Academic Press, pp. 1–22.

Piaget, J. (1967). *Biologie et Connaissance*. Paris: Gallimard.

Pias, C. (2016). *Cybernetics: The Macy Conferences 1946–1953: The Complete Transactions*. Zurich: Diaphanes.

Piccinini, G., & Craver, C. (2011). Integrating psychology and neuroscience: Functional analyses as mechanism sketches. *Synthese*, 183(3), 283–311.

Pickering, A. (2010). *The Cybernetic Brain: Sketches of Another Future*. Chicago: The University of Chicago Press.

Piekarski, M. (2023). Incorporating (variational) free energy models into mechanisms: The case of predictive processing under the free energy principle. *Synthese*, 202(2), 58.

Pouvreau, D., & Drack, M. (2007). On the history of Ludwig von Bertalanffy's "General Systemology," and on its relationship to cybernetics. *International Journal of General Systems*, 36(3), 281–337.

Rampioni, G., Mavelli, F., Damiano, L., et al. (2014). A synthetic biology approach to bio-chem-ICT: First moves towards chemical communication between synthetic and natural cells. *Natural Computing*, 13, 333–349.

Rashevsky, N. (1954). Topology and life. *Bulletin of Mathematical Biophysics*, 16, 317–348.

Rasmussen, S., Bedau, M., Hen, L., et al. (2008). *Protocells: Bridging Nonliving and Living Matter*. Cambridge, MA: MIT Press.

Rosen, R. (1970). *Dynamical System Theory in Biology: Stability Theory and Its Applications*. New York: Wiley-Interscience.

Rosen, R. (1972). Some relational cell models: The metabolism-repair systems. In R. Rosen, ed., *Foundations of Mathematical Biology: Volume II Cellular Systems*. New York: Academic Press, pp. 217–253.

Rosen, R. (1985). *Anticipatory Systems*. Oxford: Pergamon Press.

Rosen, R. (1991). *Life Itself: A Comprehensive Inquiry into the Nature, Origin, and Fabrication of Life*. New York: Columbia University Press.

Rosenblueth, A., Wiener, N., & Bigelow, J. (1943). Behaviour, purpose and teleology. *Philosophy of Science*, 10(1), 18–24.

Ruiz-Mirazo, K., Briones, C., & De la Escosura, A. (2014). Prebiotic systems chemistry: New perspectives for the origins of life. *Chemical Reviews*, 114, 285–366.

Ruiz-Mirazo, K., & Mavelli, F. (2007). Simulation model for functionalized vesicles: Lipid-peptide integration in minimal protocells. In F. Almeida e Costa, L. M. Rocha, E. Costa, I. Harvey, A. Coutinho, eds., *Advances in Artificial Life, ECAL 2007*. Berlin: Springer, pp. 32–41.

Ruiz-Mirazo, K., & Moreno, A. (2004). Basic autonomy as a fundamental step in the synthesis of life. *Artificial Life*, 10(3), 235–259.

Saborido, C., & Moreno, A. (2015). Biological pathology from an organizational perspective. *Theoretical Medicine and Bioethics*, 36(1), 83–95.

Saborido, C., Mossio, M., & Moreno, A. (2011). Biological organization and cross-generation functions. *The British Journal for the Philosophy of Science*, 62(3), 583–606.

Sachs, C. (2023). Naturalized Teleology: Cybernetics, Organization, Purpose. *Topoi*, 42(3), 781–791.

Scott-Phillips, T. C. (2009). The quest for a general account of communication: A review of sociobiology of communication. *Journal of Evolutionary Psychology*, 7(3), 245–249.

Shirt-Ediss, B., Solé, R., & Ruiz-Mirazo, K. (2013). Steady state analysis of a vesicle bioreactor with mechanosensitive channels. In P. Liò ed., *Advances in Artificial Life, ECAL 2013*. Cambridge, MA: The MIT Press, pp. 1162–1169.

Skillings, D. (2016). Holobionts and the ecology of organisms – Multi-species communities or integrated individuals? *Biology and Philosophy*, 31, 875–892.

Skillings, D. (2019). Trojan horses and black queens: "Causal core" explanations in microbiome research. *Biology & Philosophy*, 34(6), 60.

Stano, P., & Luisi, P. L. (2016). Theory and construction of semi-synthetic minimal cells. In D. L. Nesbeth, ed., *Synthetic Biology Handbook*. Boca Raton: CRC Press, pp. 209–258.

Varela, F. J. (1979). *Principles of Biological Autonomy*. New York: North-Holland.

Varela, F. J., & Maturana, H. (1972). Mechanism and biological explanation. *Philosophy of Science*, 39(3), 378–382.

Varela, F. J., Maturana, H., & Uribe, R. (1974). Autopoiesis: The organization of living systems, its characterization and a model. *Biosystems*, 5(4), 187–196.

Von Bertalanffy, L. (1968). *General System Theory*. New York: Braziller.

Walsh, D. (2015). *Organisms, Agency, and Evolution*. Cambridge: Cambridge University Press.

Weber, A., & Varela, F. J. (2002). Life after Kant: Natural purposes and the autopoietic foundations of biological individuality. *Phenomenology and the Cognitive Sciences*, 1(2), 97–125.

Wiener, N. (1948). *Cybernetics, or Control and Communication in the Animal and in the Machine*. Cambridge MA: The MIT Press.

Winning, J., & Bechtel, W. (2018). Rethinking causality in neural mechanisms: Constraints and control. *Minds and Machines*, 28(2), 287–310.

Woese, C. (2004). A new biology for a new century. *Microbiology and Molecular Biology Reviews*, 68(2),173–186.

Wolfe, C. (2014). Holism, organicism and the risk of biochauvinism. *Verifiche: Rivista di scienze umane*, 43, 39–57.

Zepik, H. H., Blöchliger, E., & Luisi, P. L. (2001). A chemical model of homeostasis. *Angewandte Chemie*, 113, 205–208.

Acknowledgments

I thank Laura Menatti for her love and support, for our discussions and collaborations, and for so many other things that listing them would easily exceed the space of an Element. The idea of writing this Element came out in a conversation with Derek Skillings, who was trying to keep me awake while I was driving during a long car trip in the south of France. I am grateful to him for encouraging me, for discussing many ideas in philosophy of biology, and for supporting me with his friendship. A substantial part of this Element was written during my guest fellowship at the KLI – Konrad Lorenz Institute for Evolution and Cognition Research (from Fall 2022 to Spring 2023). I thank the director Guido Caniglia, and all its members and fellows for the kind hospitality and for providing a very serene and stimulating research environment. I wish to thank William Bechtel for the many helpful suggestions and, together with Andrew Bollhagen and Matteo Mossio, for the very helpful feedback on a previous version of the manuscript. I thank Alvaro Moreno and all my other co-authors for the very stimulating conversations and the collaborative work, which over the years have contributed to shaping my way of thinking about living systems.

Funding

This research was supported by grant Ramón y Cajal RYC-2016–19798 funded by MCIN/AEI /10.13039/501100011033 and by ESF "Investing in your future"; by grant PID2019-104576GB-I00 for project Outonomy funded by MCIN/AEI/10.13039/501100011033; and by grant IT1668-22 funded by the Basque Government. The open access publication of this book was funded by the John Templeton Foundation (grant #62220). I deeply thank Alvaro Moreno and Derek Skillings for making these funds available from their subawards. The viewpoints expressed in this Element are those of the author and not those of the John Templeton Foundation.

Conflict of Interest

The author has no conflict of interest to declare.

Philosophy of Biology

Grant Ramsey
KU Leuven

Grant Ramsey is a BOFZAP research professor at the Institute of Philosophy, KU Leuven, Belgium. His work centers on philosophical problems at the foundation of evolutionary biology. He has been awarded the Popper Prize twice for his work in this area. He also publishes in the philosophy of animal behavior, human nature and the moral emotions. He runs the Ramsey Lab (theramseylab.org), a highly collaborative research group focused on issues in the philosophy of the life sciences.

Michael Ruse
Florida State University

Michael Ruse is the Lucyle T. Werkmeister Professor of Philosophy and the Director of the Program in the History and Philosophy of Science at Florida State University. He is Professor Emeritus at the University of Guelph, in Ontario, Canada. He is a former Guggenheim fellow and Gifford lecturer. He is the author or editor of over sixty books, most recently *Darwinism as Religion: What Literature Tells Us about Evolution*; *On Purpose*; *The Problem of War: Darwinism, Christianity, and their Battle to Understand Human Conflict*; and *A Meaning to Life*.

About the Series

This Cambridge Elements series provides concise and structured introductions to all of the central topics in the philosophy of biology. Contributors to the series are cutting-edge researchers who offer balanced, comprehensive coverage of multiple perspectives, while also developing new ideas and arguments from a unique viewpoint.

Cambridge Elements ☰

Philosophy of Biology

Printed in the United States
by Baker & Taylor Publisher Services